Lead Like A Woman - A Lady's Guide To Business Success

ISBN: 978-0-578-84427-5

Disclaimer

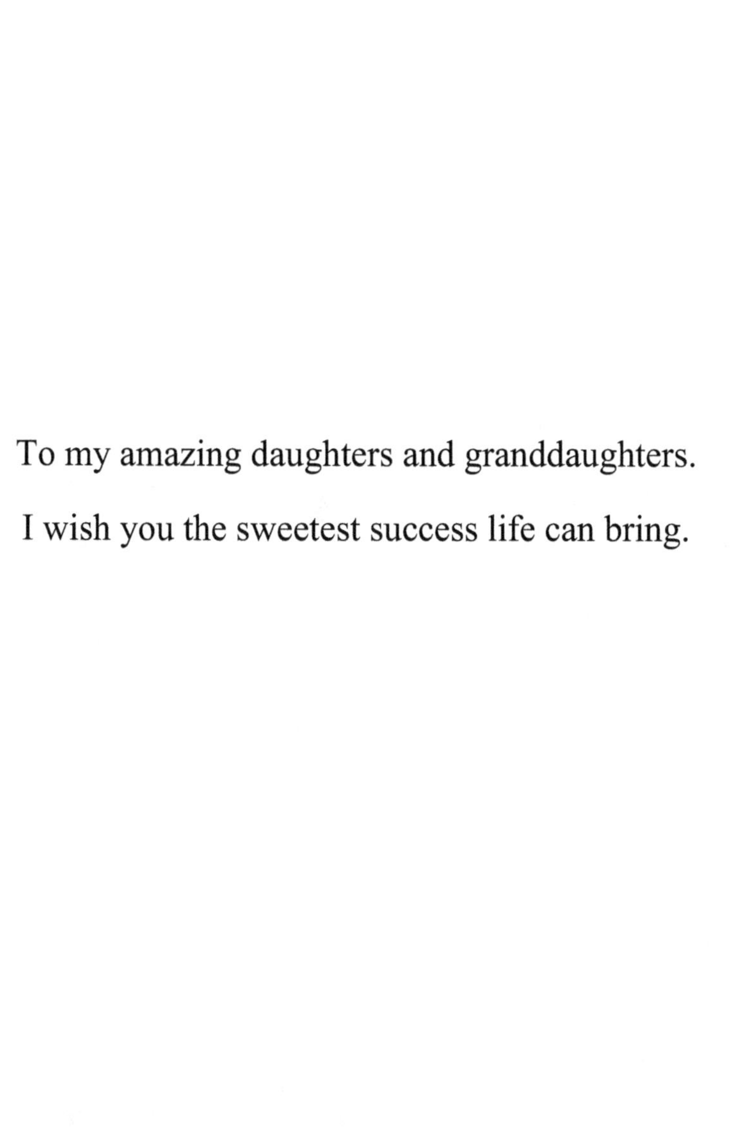

To my amazing daughters and granddaughters.

I wish you the sweetest success life can bring.

Lead Like A Woman

A Lady's Guide To Business Success

Donna J Briggs, CPA

Table of Contents

CHAPTER 1

The Power of Women in Business

"The question isn't who is going to let me; it's who is going to stop me." – Ayn Rand

I believe it has never been easier to be a woman in business than today. We have access to the business world, thanks to generations of exceptional women who opened that door to us. I deeply admire women who were brave enough to start their own business and try their luck even though they didn't have any support. They are my role models and my motivation.

One of the first female entrepreneurs was Coco Chanel. At the beginning of the twentieth century, when many women in France weren't even allowed to work, she managed to make her own revolution. And it is not just the fashion revolution I am talking about. Yes, she was the first one to dress her models in suits. She was the first one to introduce a little black dress. That's true, but those things are just a symbol of what she did for women on a bigger scale.

Coco Chanel inspired millions of women worldwide, and, using her own example, she showed them that it was possible to succeed in the business world. She is proof that there are no limits when you want to achieve something. Even when the circumstances are against you.

What are the first things that come to mind when someone mentions Coco Chanel? Glamour, courage, innovation? Maybe it's the "little black dress" or one of the most famous perfumes in the world, Chanel No 5?

Everyone's heard of Coco Chanel and her style, yet many people don't know that her life was not an easy one. She had struggles like most of us. A thing that sets her apart was her attitude that seemed to transcend the challenges. Perhaps the best way to describe her philosophy of life is in her own words: "Success is most often achieved by those who don't know that failure is inevitable."

Let's start from the beginning. Let me take you to 1883 when Gabrielle Bonheur Chanel was born. Oh, you didn't know her real name was Gabrielle? That's right. She gave herself a new name, Coco, which comes from the French slang word "cocotte", meaning kept woman. That was her nickname when she worked as a cabaret singer. That's one of the episodes from her twenties. Young Coco Chanel had to do multiple jobs to make a living and be independent. Even then, she was aware of her style and talents and knew she would make a revolution in the fashion industry.

Nevertheless, the life of this French fashion icon wasn't that straightforward. She had to prove herself time and again. Although Paris, the city of light, defined her life and career in high-end fashion, she wasn't born there. Her life story started in a less glamorous way. Most people don't know that young Coco spent most of her childhood in an orphanage in Samur, in the Loire Valley of western France. Her father, a poverty-stricken peddler, had to leave her and her four siblings there after their mother died. The orphanage was her school of life. She learned to sew very early for her age because she didn’t like plain orphanage clothes. That was a turning point in her life. As a young girl, she decided that nothing would stop her from succeeding in life.

Just like all successful people in the world, Coco Chanel started with something small. Her first business was selling elegant hats for ladies. She didn't have the means to start the business alone. Luckily, the help appeared in the form of two businessmen she became friends with. I am sure Coco didn't know about the term "networking", but she sure knew that it is important to surround yourself with the right people.

With their help, she managed to open a small hat shop on Cambon Street in Central Paris. If you go to that address today, you will see one of Chanel's most prestigious boutiques. The next time you stand in front of a Chanel boutique, try to think about how it all started. It is hard to imagine all the struggles she had to go through before she became one of the world's most famous fashion designers. Her next smart move was to open two shops in Deauville and Biarritz. Why did she choose these small towns instead of the capital city? In order to understand her decision, one needs to be familiar with that period. Coco Chanel operated during World War 1 when many Parisians fled the city to escape the German army. They found shelter in resort towns like Deauville. Parisian women didn't want to give up on their style, even in circumstances like this. Coco's shop was a life-saver and something that was bringing them joy even in the darkest times.

Years went by, and it wasn't until 1923 that she enjoyed her first massive success. That's the year when Chanel No 5 was born. Choosing the right fragrance was never an issue for Coco Chanel, who had a natural sense of both fashion and perfumes. Financing Chanel No 5 was the hard part. She knew she couldn't do it alone and that she needed to find someone to help her financially. Coco believed in her idea so much that she wasn't embarrassed to send proposals to the most famous names in the fashion industry. And her plan worked. The famous perfume-making Wertheimer family, along with Galeries Lafayette, offered to help.

The company Les Perfumes Chanel started operations a year later. Honestly, the situation was far from ideal, but she made it work. The Wertheimer family owned 70% of the venture, the owner of

Galeries Lafayette was holding 20%, and only 10% belonged to Chanel. She never stopped fighting to increase her percentage as the business grew. When her efforts to take over her own company failed, she decided to start over. During World War II, she had a connection with a German officer that allowed her to stay in her famous apartment at The Ritz. She loved the place so much, and she didn't want to leave it even during the most dangerous period. When the war finished, she had problems because of this somewhat dubious affiliation, so she decided to leave her beloved Paris and move to Switzerland.

Coco Chanel had reason to be proud and spend the rest of her life enjoying the fruits of her labor. There aren't a lot of people who create a best-selling perfume that appeals to women of every age. But she wasn't like that. Full of new ideas, she could never sit still. She breathed fashion, she lived business. When she hit 70, Coco made her fashion comeback. Again, the success didn't come immediately, yet she persisted. As a result, she made a massive impact on the fashion industry and left a lasting legacy. Her relations with the Wertheimer family improved, and Coco managed to convince them to fund her couture house. Chanel sold her business to them, and it is still in control of the Wertheimers today, making them one of the wealthiest families in France. Coco Chanel died in her famous apartment at The Ritz, where she had spent many happy years. Unlike some innovators who gained respect only after their death, Chanel enjoyed the fame and success she'd earned through all her hard work.

The designs she created are timeless, and she knew they would live long after her passing. Coco Chanel was most certainly ahead of her time. Think of the classic Chanel suit she created in 1925. Can you imagine the boldness it took to be the first designer to create a suit for women? Can you imagine the comments and the newspaper headlines at that time? She believed in her ideas and was ready to face the criticism. She knew what it took to become a true innovator. In her own words, "In order to be irreplaceable, one must always be different. The most courageous act is still to think for yourself."

As if that wasn't enough, she went on to create the "little black dress". Something the world had never seen before. At the time, it took courage to show off your legs in a short dress. But today, the "little black dress" has gained a place in every woman's closet. American Vogue compared it to the Ford motor car. There aren't a lot of products that manage to reach and maintain that level of popularity.

You and me, and all other women, we still have a lot to learn from Coco Chanel. Her approach to business is timeless, and it teaches us a few important lessons. First, believe in yourself and your ideas. Second, don't be afraid to speak up for yourself. And finally, it is never too late to start a new project, even if you are 70 years old.

You Are Fearfully and Wonderfully Made

Some of you may know Psalm 139:14 that says you are "fearfully and wonderfully made". It is one of the most inspiring passages I've ever read. You were created to be exactly you! It's all about the uniqueness and strengths you have. You are born with unique talents, and you should use them to inspire others and to make the world a better place. Don't waste your talents trying to fit in with a world that wants to stifle individuality.

I don't understand why so many women strive to be the same as everybody else. There's no point. We are all different, and that's what makes life so beautiful! Why would you try to be the same as other businesspeople? Why would you compare yourself with someone else of either sex? No one is perfect. Everyone has their strengths and their weaknesses. Successful people have learned how to get the most out of their strengths. The only way to be really successful and fulfilled is to play to those strengths. That's what this book is all about. I want to show you how to get the most out of every situation, by playing to your strengths and relying on your unique talents.

What Makes Women So Powerful in Business?

In previous decades, business principles have changed a lot. One of the most important things that determines success in business is interpersonal skills. People are finally realizing their importance. It seems that everybody is talking about them these days. And the good news is that you have them, although you may not be aware of them yet. Think about that for a second. You've been developing interpersonal skills for years. We're social beings, and we crave interactions. Every conversation is a chance to learn something new and improve your skills. You are using these skills daily to nurture your relationships or solve personal problems. You are using them at home, or with your friends, or even with strangers you communicate with.

It's time to take it to the next level and play to your strengths. Instead of focusing on what you don't have, focus on the strengths that every woman has. For example, empathy. Implementing only that skill can be a game-changer for your business. And think about what could happen if you learned how to get the most out of all those skills that you already have. Whether you are a business owner, or a manager, focusing on your strengths can help you multiply your results. Let's look at the key strengths women have in a business setting and how to get the most out of them.

Relationship Building

Business is all about building lasting relationships with your customers and your colleagues. Cultivating relationships takes time, and so many business people focus on other matters. They believe that they have other priorities, such as reports or deadlines. They forget that business is about people. You can't do business without people. You should focus on building lasting business relationships, and I know you can do it. You may wonder how I know that. Well, I know you are doing a great job cultivating relationships with your friends and family. You should apply the same approach to business, and you will get fantastic results. Many studies show that women have a unique leadership approach. For us, it's all about building great teams and empowering others. Women instinctively know that the only way to lift themselves is by lifting others. That is a great way to build lasting success.

Amazing Communication Skills

Women are excellent communicators and negotiators. According to Forbes, our top three strengths in communication are:

- Understanding body language and nonverbal cues
- Being good listeners
- Extending empathy

All of them are essential for success. Men often lack these skills, especially showing empathy. The reason for that is that society has told them that they should not openly express their emotions. As a result, women are usually better at showing empathy and understanding other people. Some women think that empathy doesn't help in business, but that's just a common misconception. If you treat people well, you will gain their respect and support. Listening skills can help you a lot, too. Not only do people appreciate a good listener, but you will get to know what others don't. Women are also better at verbalizing their thoughts and feelings. We've been practicing it since an early age, and we're able to explain our ideas clearly and concisely.

High Emotional Intelligence

Emotional intelligence is very complex, and some people believe it may be even more important than our IQ. It is a combination of social skills, empathy, and self-awareness. Women usually have high emotional intelligence that allows them to understand the emotions of others as well as their own. It helps women solve complex problems at work. Empathy is particularly important for business leaders. It promotes understanding and helps create solutions for the good of everyone. Never underestimate the power of emotional intelligence. You can use it to build fantastic relationships and get great results.

Problem Solving

According to one study, female leaders are more assertive and persuasive than their male counterparts. What's more, we're more willing to take risks. Women are problem-solving oriented, both in professional and private life. We're used to devising innovative solutions, and we need to take that to the next level. You may not be aware of this skill, but I know you are using it daily. Another thing that gives us an advantage is that we're open to discussion. I sincerely believe in honesty and collaboration. Talking (really talking) with colleagues and customers can help you gain new insights.

You will see matters from different perspectives which may inspire you to come up with unique solutions.

Your Woman-Owned Business – Getting Certified

If you are like most women, you might have doubts about getting your "woman-owned business" certified. You may have heard that it is a long process, and you are unsure whether it is worth it. From my experience, it's one of the best ways to get more visibility and, possibly, more business. We're lucky to be living in a world that encourages female entrepreneurs. There are more opportunities now than ever before, you just have to know where to look for them.

Certifications can open doors, making you eligible for government contracts. If that's your goal, I'd suggest getting certified as soon as possible. But that's not all. Did you know that many companies have initiatives to work with female-owned businesses? Some of the companies from that list are giants like Starbucks and Target. How does that sound to you? Moreover, certifications can allow you to become part of the community and use resources such as education programs.

There are multiple ways to get a certification, a great place to start is the Small Business Administration. Let me explain why in more detail. The first certification I want to discuss is a women-owned small business (WOSB) certification. All women can benefit from it, especially those interested in federal contracts and resources. The Small Business Administration provides training and counseling. This allows you to apply for federal contracts, as well as credit and capital. Most importantly, they can guide you through the process. I know how hard it can be when you are starting your own business. Everything seems new and a bit scary, and if your friends aren't entrepreneurs, you don't have anyone to talk to. The Small Business Administration offers that kind of support for new entrepreneurs like you. Businesses that reach out to the SBA have a much better success rate than those without that kind of help. Everything is easier when you have someone to guide you along the way.

So, what does it take to obtain a WOSB certification?

First, your business has to meet the small business size standards found in the Code of Federal Regulations. Your business should primarily operate in the United States. Also, it should make a significant contribution to the United States economy. Second, female U.S. citizens have to be owners of at least 51% of the business. In order to apply, you should hold the highest officer position in your company. You should be responsible for making long-term, business-related decisions. Moreover, your responsibility should also be managing day-to-day operations. Finally, you have to work at your business full-time, during regular working hours.

Even a start-up company should consider this. There are no waiting periods for requesting a certification. Meaning, there's no rule regarding how long your business has been operational in order to be eligible. You can apply whenever you want! What's more, I know many women who applied in the very early phases of their business. All of them said that it was one of the best decisions they ever made, as they got a lot of new opportunities.

One lesser-known option is the economically-disadvantaged women-owned small business (EDWOSB) certification. It's similar to the WOSB certification, but it also presents new opportunities for contracts and resources.

What's the difference then, and why should you bother obtaining it?

The most significant difference is that there's less competition in the EDWOSB sector. Why? Does that mean that all business owners are well-off? Not at all! Well, that's not how they started at least. The thing is that a lot of women never hear about EDWOSB certification. Often, they think that they won't get it, and that's why they don't even apply! I suggest you try as there are no negative consequences. If you are unsuccessful, you can opt for another certification. But if you recognize yourself in the following paragraph, you should definitely go for it.

The requirements for EDWOSB certification include all requirements for the WOSB certification and more. There are three main financial requirements. First, your personal net worth should be less than $750,000. Before you dismiss this option, let me explain. Equity in your business and primary personal residence don't count in this number. Nor does income from a limited liability company or S corporation that you reinvested or used to pay taxes related to the business. Finally, even the funds from your retirement account don't count, in most cases. The second rule is that adjusted gross income averaged over three years has to be a maximum of $350,000. Again, the good thing is that any funds you reinvested or used to pay business taxes don't count here. The third and final requirement is that the fair market value of all assets has to be a maximum of $6 million. Excluding funds from your retirement account.

Let's consider how it all works once you get a certification. Let's say that some businesses want to work with a female-owned company. They will send a request to the Small Business Administration asking them to provide a list of female-owned companies. As you can see, many opportunities never become public, as they find partners this way. The main principle is similar for WOSB and EDWOSB. But fewer businesses qualify as EDWOSB, which means there's less competition. Therefore, your chances of getting the contract are much higher. That's why I suggest applying for that one as well. There's nothing to lose. And the benefits could be enormous. I am not just talking about financial help. For me, it's also about meeting new people, getting support, and learning more about business.

Of course, every state has additional initiatives for female business owners. They may be worth your attention. Focus on getting your federal certification first, and then consider the other options available. The good thing is that you can apply to multiple programs, as there are few restrictions.

Getting Paid What You are Worth

Many women struggle when they have to ask for a raise or negotiate compensation. They instinctively devalue themselves by thinking that no one is going to pay them that much. But that's not true. There are proven negotiation techniques to achieve the conditions you want. It all starts with your mindset. If you don't believe you are worth it, you won't have the self-confidence to convince others.

You are not alone. Even women in the highest positions, such as CEOs, sometimes struggle with their self-worth. When you learn to overcome it, everything will change for you. So, the first step is to convince yourself that you are worth it. And I know you are because of all the effort you've put into mastering your skills. You may need to remind yourself for a while until it becomes your default mindset. Then, when it's time to negotiate your compensation, you can use these five proven tips to increase your likelihood of success.

Raise Your Expectations

The only way to do more, become more, and earn more is to start thinking big. The first step is to raise your expectations. Most women settle for less than they know they deserve. We're afraid to speak up for ourselves, and we don't want to sound as if we're boasting about our achievements. It is something in our upbringing that's been telling us that we should not ask for more. One study confirmed that it is true – women settle for less. They trained both men and women in negotiation strategies. Women knew all the tips and tricks. And yet, they ended up with less money than men from the same group. The reason was that their expectations weren't high enough, and they didn't insist on what they wanted.

Inform Yourself

Do you know what your market value is? Do you know what the average pay for a position like yours is? If you are not sure, it is time to do your research. Consider this scenario that often happens to great employees. Your employers are happy with your work, and they want to give you a raise. They ask you how much you want. You ask for an amount that is under market and they happily agree. Research that is backed with facts prevails and is your best friend.

Keep Track of Your Achievements

Don't assume that your manager will see how much you've done for the company and reward you accordingly. Instead, keep track of your achievements and mention them when the time is right. Numbers don't lie. Maybe you've generated many sales and deserve a bonus. On the other hand, perhaps you helped the company save a lot of money, which is also essential. If you show what you bring to the table, it is hard to dismiss your requests.

Fake It Until You Make It

If you don't feel confident, that's normal. It can be scary to request a raise, and there's always a fear of rejection. However, conceal your nerves and uncertainty. If necessary, practice your speech beforehand with someone you can trust. Try to appear confident and see how their behavior towards you changes. People will start respecting you more, and as a result, your salary will grow accordingly.

Get Out of Your Comfort Zone

Success starts when you leave your comfort zone. If you are not ready to do it at work, you can practice by challenging yourself in other areas. Learn a new skill, take a class, or sign up for a marathon. With each change, your confidence and self-worth will grow. Then, you will start feeling more confident at work as well.

You Are More Powerful Than You Think

Women are more powerful as leaders and business owners than they realize. All you have to do is change your mindset and open yourself up to that option. Your first job is to convince yourself that you can do it. That's the hardest part. Convincing others is much easier once you know who you really are. You should play to your strengths and tap into your resources. By resources, I mean concepts we've discussed in this chapter like social skills, emotional intelligence, and problem-solving. There are many other skills that you don't realize you can use in business. Instead of focusing on your flaws, focus on your strengths from now on.

If you could remember only one idea from this book, I'd want it to be that you were born to achieve great things. Everything starts with the right mindset. I once read somewhere that a woman with the right attitude can conquer the world, and I fully believe it. I know that you have that potential within yourself. Otherwise, you wouldn't be reading this book. In the next chapter, I will share insight from my own career.

CHAPTER 2

Who Am I

"Success doesn't come from what you do occasionally. It comes from what you do consistently." – Marie Forleo

When I hear someone's advice, I want to know who that person is and why they are qualified to advise me. And I suggest that you do the same. I believe that results often speak louder than words. That's why I am happy to let my results do the talking for me. I've been in the financial industry for more than 30 years, and I am a trusted financial advisor to numerous clients. In this book, I want to share with you the most important insights I've learned during my long career. I want to be of service to you and share all of my knowledge.

Today, I am a shareholder and Principal of Coker James & Company, P.C. As a leading business advisory firm, we help our clients grow wealth and preserve it. Simply put, I help people secure their financial future, and I enjoy every aspect of it. I am a Certified Public Accountant and hold both an Insurance License and a Securities License. My areas of expertise include taxation, financial planning, and financial accounting.

I grew up in the suburbs of Atlanta, Georgia. My education includes an undergraduate degree in Accounting and a Masters of Taxation, both from Georgia State University. My education didn't stop there. I believe that we have to keep learning and growing, especially in industries like mine where rules often change. My credentials come with annual education requirements, which keep you abreast of the latest news and changes in the field. Some people may say that those requirements are pretty high. But I believe that the only way to be good at what you do is by investing your time in constant learning.

I strongly believe in the power of knowledge. I've always thought of education as something that can open many doors. But you have to go through them and do the best you can with what you have.

You may wonder what qualifies me to tell you how to succeed in your business or how to rise up the ladder in the industry. It is my 30-year-long career and all the clients I've helped with financial decisions and achieving their goals. After all the formal education and credentials, I can confidently say that my clients and colleagues have been the greatest teachers. Every case, every problem solved, every challenge comes with a lesson learned.

Whatever challenge you might be facing, someone has walked there before. I am looking very forward to sharing many things I have learned over the years. That is the aim of this book. I want to be generous in sharing my knowledge and experiences with others. If I can help someone who struggles with the financial aspect of starting their own business, or the challenges of climbing the corporate ladder, then I've accomplished my mission.

There's Nothing New Under the Sun

Biblical King Solomon knew something that people still can't accept. He was one of the wisest and richest men that had ever lived. He wrote the famous quote: "There's nothing new under the sun." It's all about foundational truths. There's nothing in the world that hasn't already happened or that we haven't seen before. Things exist, and people exist in the ways they always have. Some attributes like confidence, risk-taking initiative, and a great work ethic never go out of fashion. Technologies may change, but the principle is the same. The sooner you accept that, the faster you will be able to move forward in your business.

I never liked business books that promise to offer some new magical formula. There's no such thing as a quick fix or a cheesy gimmick. I believe in foundational truths that people have been using for centuries to build something out of their lives. Being a good leader, having a willingness to learn, and a work ethic is the only formula you will ever need. A strong mind and a soft heart are the recipes for greatness in life.

The Starting Point – Focus on the Big Picture

We all start with big plans and great ideas, but it can be easy to get lost in the process. Women tend to focus on the details, and that's fantastic, but we should not let the details distract us from the big picture. How is it possible to manage a business without focusing on everyday details, you may ask. Of course, I am not suggesting you ignore the details. After all, the small actions are what get you from where you are now to where you want to be.

Details add up over time and grow into big advances. Even if you go slowly, one step at a time, your actions will add up, and you will suddenly realize how far you've come. But remember to take a step back every now and then to take a look at the bigger picture. This is essential – to remind yourself about your goals and why you started. The big picture is what keeps you going, even when you are going through tough times in your career or your business.

It can be easy to get lost in daily, repetitive tasks. If you are stressed out and bored, you may ask yourself why you are even doing this. You may start doubting whether it is really worth it. That's the right moment to switch your focus from the details that may be bothering you to the big picture. One of the best ways to do so is to delegate tasks that take too much time. Women often try to do everything alone, but that's not possible. That's the surest way to get to the point of burnout. As your business grows, you will have to delegate some tasks. And when you find the right person to do them, you will realize it's one of the best things you've done for yourself and your business! Not only will you have more time to focus on tasks that matter most, but your mind will also be calmer and more creative.

Ultimately, success comes down to setting your goals and plotting a course towards them. And when you make a plan, persevere. A lot of unplanned situations will occur along the way, and you will have to manage them. However, don't become overwhelmed with the details you face in the process. Take the time to handle them, but don't let them change your direction. Never forget where you are heading.

Simple Principles Create Great Results

I think you can understand my business philosophy by now. There's no magic pill, just time-proven principles that can help you achieve your goals. The sooner you realize that, the less time it will take you to raise your business or your career to the level of your dreams. I do believe in doing the right things and focusing on the fundamental pillars of success. Everything starts from there. Some of the principles may even seem too simple, and you might be tempted to skip them. But the point is always to give it your best. Don't take anything I say for granted. Instead, try it yourself. If you implement these principles daily, you will achieve the success you desire.

There are no shortcuts to success, but I have some tips that can make your ride to the business of your dreams easier and smoother. In the following chapters, I will focus on the exact principles that can help you elevate your game.

CHAPTER 3

The Forefront of Your Mind

"Whatever we plant in our subconscious mind and nourish with repetition and emotion will one day become a reality." – Earl Nightingale

If you asked me what's the most important ingredient for success – I'd say that everything starts with your mindset. I know that having your goals at the forefront of your mind makes more difference than anything else you could possibly do. Success doesn't happen overnight. It is a result of dedication and focusing on what you want. All successful people have this particular approach to life where they keep their goals at the forefront of their minds. That way, they won't forget about them, and they stay focused. And if you don't have this mindset yet, don't worry. Your way of thinking is just a habit, and like any other habit, you can change it. High achievers are those who've developed habits and disciplines that lead them down the road to success.

Let me tell you one fun story to explain how our minds work. A couple of years ago, I decided to buy a 1998 Jeep Wrangler. Shocking, I know. I am the type of businesswoman who drives a black, four-door sedan. A Jeep Wrangler isn't something that's typical for me. But I felt adventurous, and I wanted a recreational vehicle. So, I guess my Jeep was my play toy. Besides, it was very affordable, and I fell in love with it. But you know what happened next? The moment I got the Jeep, I saw Jeeps everywhere. People started talking to me about them. I met other people who are passionate about Jeeps. I encountered the "Jeep wave". The reason I noticed them everywhere was that they were at the forefront of my mind.

I am sure this has happened to you at least once. I did a bit of research, and I found out there's a name for this phenomenon! In this chapter, I will explain it in more detail.

The Baader-Meinhof Phenomenon

Has your friend ever showed you a new dress in an unusual color, and you started noticing clothing of the same color everywhere? I am certain you know what I mean. When you suddenly start seeing something everywhere, your brain plays a trick on you. I learned that the name for this is Baader-Meinhof phenomenon. The other term for it is *frequency illusion*, and it is one type of cognitive bias. Put simply, cognitive bias happens when your mind doesn't think rationally. Instead, it starts creating new patterns that sometimes don't make sense. Arnold Zwicky, a linguist from Stanford University, coined the term *frequency illusion* in 2006. He said it is a combination of two processes that can happen at the same time: selective attention and confirmation bias.

Selective attention often occurs when you learn something new. Suddenly, you start seeing it everywhere. You may think that something around you has changed, but the only one who has changed is you. Your brain is paying more attention to that thing than to anything else you see daily. Before, it didn't exist for you because you weren't aware of it. You think it's new to the whole world, when in fact, you are the only one noticing it. Learning new things transforms your brain. Learning can change your perception, and that's why it is essential to always increase your learning, especially in business.

Cognitive bias? Selective attention? Yes, please! I want to absolutely choose the items I keep at the forefront of my mind! As the following chapters of this book unfold, imagine if your subconscious mind focused on your execution strategy. Or on being a leader, leveraging your work life, selling and serving with success, and accumulating wealth in the process. Building that into the fabric of your life changes your perspective and your outcome.

Becoming a Lifelong Learner – The Ten Habits You Must Develop

"The capacity to learn is a gift; The ability to learn is a skill; The willingness to learn is a choice." – Brian Herbert

Just because your formal education ended, it doesn't mean you should stop learning. In fact, self-education is often more important than your university degrees. Take me as an example. I graduated years ago. After that, there were a lot of changes in my field, as they occur in all areas. If I'd stopped learning the day I got my degree, I wouldn't be able to help my clients today. My job requires learning new things all the time, and that's what I love about it. I see it as a challenge and an opportunity to grow. We've never had access to more information than today, and it would be a shame to miss out on it. Also, our world is changing very fast, and you have to learn and adapt if you want to stay at the top of your game. We're living in the middle of a digital revolution which requires us to adapt faster than any previous generation. In this section, I want to introduce to you the concept of lifelong learning. The most successful people I've ever met are continually growing and learning. They have an open mindset that helps them use every opportunity to learn.

This approach to life has many benefits, and I will name just some of them here. First, if you commit to constant learning, you will become an expert in your field. The more knowledge you have, the smarter decisions you will be able to make. You will get more insights, and you will have more ideas on improving your business. Second, this approach will bring you many new opportunities. You may become passionate about something you never heard of before. You may take up new hobbies or meet people who can help with your business. You may even start a completely different career that maybe hadn't even existed when you graduated. Finally, lifelong learners keep their minds sharp and train their focus. They feel years younger than those who stop learning and settle down. They have a more optimistic approach to life. It can also help you maintain a healthy, active life.

Lifelong learning is simpler than you may have thought. Below, I will list ten habits that could change your life. Of course, you can modify them to see what works for you best.

Learn Something New Every Day

Don't worry as this doesn't mean that you have to spend hours learning new skills daily. But once you get the attitude of a lifelong learner, learning new things will become natural to you. You are probably already learning a lot of stuff every day although you may not be aware of it. For instance, you could learn something new while reading a magazine, talking to a friend, or even scrolling through social media. But if you surround yourself with inspiring people, you will have more chances to learn. This often happens spontaneously in conversation about ordinary stuff. Someone will mention something you've never heard before. Maybe it is a new word or some new concept. You may feel uncomfortable asking people to explain it to you, although you should not be. I hear new concepts from my colleagues and my clients, and I am never afraid to ask for an explanation. However, if you are, you can always google it. That's the blessing of living in the modern, technological world. All knowledge is just one click away from us.

Read a Lot

If you could implement only one new habit in your life, I'd suggest you go with daily reading. The most famous entrepreneurs and CEOs read for at least 30 minutes every day. If they have time for it, then so should you. I've found so many life-changing ideas in books. People who don't read books are missing out. I don't suggest reading only business books. You can read anything you like, as you can find advice and inspiration in the most unexpected places. Scripture, biographies, psychological books, even poetry. Some people prefer to read first thing in the morning, while their day is still fresh. But you should find what works best for you. Everything depends on your schedule and your routines. Reading before going to sleep has many benefits as well. It is a great way to get some food for thought that your brain can process unconsciously.

Set Learning Goals

Successful people love setting goals in all areas of their life. Why should learning be an exception? The only way to know whether you are growing is to measure your progress. The best way to do so is to set clear, realistic goals for every area of your life. Many people claim that they love reading and learning, but when you ask them when they last read a book, they can't remember. They are genuinely shocked because they love reading, but it is easy to forget about it if it is not on your schedule. Learning goals will keep you on track whenever you want to quit. Also, they are an excellent motivation and a source of fulfillment. I suggest you set monthly learning goals. They can include anything: courses you want to take, books you want to read, skills you want to practice, etc.

Have Different Hobbies

Business people sometimes think that hobbies are a waste of time. They couldn't be more wrong! First, everyone needs a rest from time to time. It is much better to spend your free time doing something you like as a hobby than endlessly scrolling through social media. Hobbies also allow you to meet new people and grow your circle of friends. But the most important thing is that you learn so much without even realizing it. Choose a hobby you enjoy and that helps you relax. It can be anything really – art, gardening, dance. With time, you will learn a new skill before you know it! The new skills you acquire are very important. Many skills are transversal, which means you can use them in different fields. Your hobby can actually help you become better at your work. Also, famous people say that they often get the best business ideas while doing something that relaxes them.

Attend Courses Regularly

Today there are so many convenient online courses that you can't say you don't have enough time for learning. It is easier than ever before to keep your knowledge current. Online courses give you the freedom to access them whenever you want. You can customize it according to your schedule. If you want to be successful in any field, you should set a goal to attend some courses every year. But apart from your industry, I suggest you also attend classes on business, economy, leadership, and other essential topics that inspire you.

If you've never attended an online course before, feel free to explore some options. There are many websites offering courses. Even some of the best universities in the U.S. offer courses for free. Maybe you hadn't had a chance to go to Harvard, but you can now access some of their courses from your home. Previous generations didn't have this opportunity, so make sure to use it.

Learn New Skills

The most successful people in the world are always learning something new. Learning a new skill is a great way to keep your mind sharp, no matter what age you are. If you are not sure where to start, it can be a good idea to learn a new language. By doing so, you are also challenging your brain and learning important aspects of other cultures. If you've always wanted to learn French, why don't you start now? Remember, it is never too late to learn a new skill. Many people decide to enroll in a university or change their career in their fifties. I think that's fantastic, and you can use them as inspiration. On the other hand, other people like to learn more practical skills. Learning how to bake or trying out new recipes can be as stimulating for your brain as playing chess.

Use Every Chance to Grow

As I mentioned, your goal should be to develop a lifelong learner attitude. Chances to learn and grow are all around us, but so many people don't see them. Lifelong learners actively seek opportunities to grow and learn new things. Instead of watching TV shows like other people, they watch documentaries or inspiring interviews. They use every available chance to grow. They visit cultural events, museums, and concerts. I am sure there are many events in your local community. If you are one of those women who see ads for such events, want to go but realize you don't have time, you need to change something. Organize your time according to your priorities. And remember that the time you dedicate to learning and exploring is never wasted time.

Listen to Audiobooks and Podcasts

If you spend most of your day at work and commuting, you may not have time to read. However, that's not an excuse anymore. Today, most books are available in audio format, so you can listen to them whenever you want. Many women prefer audiobooks to paper. They can listen to them while driving, exercising, or doing housework. That way, you can go through hundreds of pages in a week, which might be difficult otherwise. Another option is listening to podcasts. Their popularity is growing every day, and so many people now have their own podcast. That means that you have to choose very carefully. Not all podcasts are great, but if you pick a quality podcast by a famous author or an entrepreneur, you can learn a great deal.

Get Out of That Comfort Zone

If you work in one industry for decades, it gets easy to settle down. Complacency is your enemy. You are already an expert in your field, and you know more than most other people in the area. However, that doesn't make you an expert in everything. There's always something new to learn and discover. Getting out of your comfort zone every now and then will help shift your perspective. Even though you may be a senior in your field, for a moment, you will feel like a beginner starting something new. Everything seems unfamiliar and scary, but it is also exciting at the same time. There are so many ways to get out of your comfort zone. Maybe you can start learning about digital technologies and the way you could implement them in your industry. Alternatively, becoming an educator is also a way to leave your zone of comfort. You can sign up to give lectures to students or to be a mentor to someone new in your industry. Why not be one of those people with their own podcast?

Know It's Never Too Late

I see many women starting college in their forties and fifties, and I think that's beautiful! I want you to remember it is never too late to learn something you always wanted. Maybe you are an entrepreneur, but you always wanted to study nutrition. Go for it! Don't let your fears stop you. Young students admire people who decide to continue studying. However, this advice isn't only about learning. It is never too late to start over. If you've had a great business idea for years, why don't you try to develop it now? It's time to get rid of limiting beliefs. It is better to start late than to never start at all and live with regrets. You never know what it can turn out to be. Maybe you will develop a new business, a side project, and meet inspiring people along the way. Hello! Martha Stewart rose to popularity when her first book hit the shelves in her forties.

Start with Changing Your Attitude

I hope that this chapter showed you the importance of having the right attitude. Open yourself up to this idea. Accept that there's still a lot you have to learn. Some people panic when they realize they will have to keep learning forever. But I love it. I see it as an opportunity to improve myself and my skills. The concept of lifelong learning has never been more critical than today. Knowledge is more available than it has ever been before. You just have to make an effort and decide to learn something new. The good thing is that it will soon become natural for you. When you develop this habit, you will start seeking opportunities to grow every day. And that's when everything will start changing for you and your business. Never underestimate the power of your mind. What you focus on can shape your outcomes. When you understand this, you can use it to your advantage. In the next chapter, I will keep talking about your mind, but in a different, more practical way, providing some useful tips you can apply immediately.

CHAPTER 4

Strategic Thinking Creates Success

"Things don't just happen, they are made to happen."
– John F. Kennedy

I am going to give you one real-life example of a problem-solving attitude. I had an interesting conversation with a lady executive who runs a $15 million company. She wanted to expand her market share, but that required sending a significant number of her staff to another state. It all happened during the global pandemic, which made the situation even more difficult. One day she told me: "I just got off the phone with my operational team, and I just can't believe that these men can't think outside the box." This intrigued me, so I asked her to explain. It turned out that they were one step away from signing the contract, but the operational team had to travel and do it in person. The hotels weren't open, so they told her that they couldn't go. I asked her: "What did you do?" And she replied: "I told them: 'Guys, rent an RV and drive to the customer!'" It was such a simple solution, but no one thought of it!

When someone mentions a problem-solving attitude, people may think of life-changing decisions. In fact, it is more about solving the daily challenges you encounter along the way. Solutions are often far simpler than we expect them to be. Yet, you have to learn to think that way, and then they will come naturally to you.

Science has proven that female and male brains function in a different way. That can be a great advantage for us, even though men still dominate the business world. We all know that women are better at multitasking, but do you know why? Our hormones may play a big part. Some studies show that our high levels of estrogen help us multitask and perform better than men when we're under pressure. Also, when making a decision, we tend to consider the bigger picture and all parties involved. This could be a serious competitive advantage in the business world. Therefore, you should not try to act like a man. Act like a lady, and get the most out of your strengths!

The Qualities of Amelia Earhart - Let's Be Her!

"Decide whether or not the goal is worth the risks involved. If it is, stop worrying." – Amelia Earhart

I've always admired brave women who were ahead of their time. One of them is American aviation pioneer Amelia Earhart. She set an example for women of her era, but also for the generations to come. She is still one of the bravest American women in history. I admire her because when she set herself a goal, nothing could stop her. She showed the world that women could accomplish anything that men could. If she did that at the beginning of the twentieth century, think about what we could achieve now?

However, I believe that her success wasn't just an anomaly. She was brilliant, and she had all the qualities necessary for success. There wasn't much literature on goal setting back then, so I guess she had extraordinary natural capabilities. Let's take a look at the qualities that helped her achieve her goals and how you can obtain those qualities too.

Confidence

Nothing would have been possible without her great self-confidence. Even when the whole world said that she couldn't do something, she believed that she could. And she did it. She made solo flights across the Pacific and the Atlantic Ocean. Something that was unprecedented and dangerous, even for a man at the time. But she did it. In the beginning, she didn't have much support. She realized that she'd have to be her greatest supporter and believe in herself unconditionally. Not only did this help her accomplish all her goals, but it also helped her make a start in the first place.

Dedication and Hard Work

Amelia Earhart wasn't born a pilot. Nor is anyone else. It took years of dedication and hard work until she reached the level of skill she needed. She could have given up many times, but she didn't. She persisted. Amelia wanted to be a pilot from an early age. But that wasn't her first job. She couldn't afford the equipment. She had to work hard for a couple of years until she earned the money she needed to support herself. No rich family. No rich husband. She managed everything on her own.

Focus

Flying alone requires a lot of focus. If you let anything distract you, it may be fatal. Take this as a metaphor. If you really want to achieve something, that goal deserves your exclusive attention. Amelia was a hero, but even she wasn't an expert in multiple fields. Choose your goals wisely and then stick to them. Focus is essential both for short-term and long-term goals, and focusing on the bigger picture may help when you get distracted.

Leadership

You don't have to manage a company of 100 people to become a leader. Leadership is something that occurs when you have to stand up for yourself and others. Amelia Earhart was a leader because she organized her flights alone. She didn't wait for someone to tell her what to do. She flew solo and also managed the people around her. Most of them were men, more experienced than her and with more technical knowledge. But they lacked leadership skills. I've met great leaders who were managing small teams of five people. I've also met CEOs of large organizations who lacked any leadership skills. Leadership doesn't have anything to do with your title or net worth. It's about your character.

Risk-Taking

I believe that you can't accomplish anything worthwhile without taking a risk. Amelia Earhart was a bit extreme because, at the time, she didn't have all the equipment that we have today. But she is a good example of a woman who wasn't afraid to take a risk. Do you know that she didn't have the exact coordinates of her flight? With today's modern technology, this is hard to appreciate. Can you imagine the courage it took to fly relying on instinct?

Egoless

People who knew her personally recall that she was very modest and that she never bragged about her accomplishments. She let her deeds speak for themselves. The most successful people in the world are often very humble. But what does it have to do with goal setting? Well, people who always brag about what they are going to do are usually those who don't do anything. They don't have clear goals, and they just talk rather than act. Amelia Earhart had her plans, and she didn't waste time bragging about what she would do next.

Passion

Today, many people choose their careers based on salary and recognition. Especially in the airline industry, where employees are well-paid. That's the worst way to set your goals. You may accomplish them, but you may also lose motivation along the way. Because those goals were never what you "really" wanted. Amelia chose a career she was passionate about. She didn't know whether or not she would become rich and famous. Yes, you should set your goals using your mind, but don't ignore what your heart wants.

Determination

Amelia had to go through numerous attempts that ended with failure until she succeeded. Her determination was the only thing that kept her going. Setting goals may be the easier part. The hard part is sticking to them even when you aren't winning. Whenever you fail, remember why you started in the first place. Whenever you fall, pick yourself up and start over. This may be one of the most challenging processes in life. Amelia was aware of that, but she persisted. And that's why she eventually achieved the goals she set.

Goal Setting Is One of the Most Import Things You Do

Now, I want to talk about one of my very favorite things in the entire world: goal setting. Setting goals is, by far, one of the most important aspects of your professional and financial life. There are a lot of books on the subject, and I know you've heard this many times. But I want to repeat that without goals, and budgets, and strategies, and concepts in which we report to ourselves and others, you cannot be successful.

Think about this example: Weight Watchers model. They have the most fundamental diet plan in the world, nothing super fancy. And they've been wildly successful because they force you to set goals, record your outcome, and be accountable to other people. There's no magic in that formula. What they have are formality and structure. If you are already into goal-setting and list-making, I believe you can take it to the next level. If you haven't done so before, it may be the time to start. Neglecting this aspect can have serious consequences in all areas of your life.

Let's review the way we set goals and monitor them, particularly in the financial world. I am a big fan of Michael Hyatt's full focus planner. You can learn about his methods in his books and podcasts. If you don't embrace his process, any similar process on the market will give you similar traction. And whatever you are doing now, if you can increase it by 10 to 20% in this area, start there. If you are a great planner and you are methodical, and you track things, and you think you are on top of your financial world, expand it, kick it up. I really encourage you to do this. And the reason is, we're going to talk a lot about strategic thinking.

Let's get this straight: you can't think strategically if you don't have a strategy. We're going to talk about how you make good business decisions. We're going to talk about making plans that are multi-generational plans for the future. No magic pills, no winning lottery tickets. The reason it is so incredibly important to develop goals is that you can't monitor what you don't develop. You can't monitor and change and learn from what you haven't planned. Whatever method you choose, you need a five to ten-year goal, especially in your financial planning. You need a one-year annual goal, and you need to break it down into smaller goals. However, setting goals is just the first part. The other part is about changing the way you think.

Think Critically and Strategically

Many people don't know the difference between critical and strategic thinking. I will use this opportunity to draw a distinction between the two. When we think of strategic thinking, we usually think of a business setting and creating long-term plans. It focuses on the future, envisioning outcomes, and creating strategies to succeed. It is essential for ensuring that your business keeps its competitive advantage. On the other hand, critical thinking is a tool you can use along the way. Critical thinking is essential for problem-solving, decision-making, and negotiating.

Strategic thinking is essential for writing your business plan. Don't forget to include both mid-term and long-term goals in your business plan. Your business plan isn't something you should rush. The goal isn't just to write something. Your goal should be to write a strategic framework that shows what you have to do in order to achieve your goals. To sum it up: you should use strategic thinking when outlining your goals and plans. However, even the best business plans have some flaws. That's where critical thinking helps. You should rely on it to solve any issues that may occur along the way and that you weren't able to predict.

The Big Mindset Barrier – The Fear of Failure

"Failing isn't bad when you learn what not to do."
– Albert Einstein

Let me tell you a story of a woman who wasn't afraid of failure. After every defeat, she started over, having gained valuable insights. And eventually, she succeeded and became the first female billionaire author ever. I am talking about J.K. Rowling, of course. It took her almost a decade to publish her first book, but she achieved the kind of success she couldn't have imagined in her wildest dreams. And certainly not when she was an unemployed, single mother struggling to feed her child. But let's start from the beginning.

She was a young woman when she first got the idea to write a children's book about wizards. She started full of enthusiasm but, after a couple of months, her mother died. This led her to depression and, naturally, she wasn't able to concentrate on writing. Although she had to postpone her dream of becoming a writer, she never forgot about it. It was still there, waiting for the right moment. J.K. Rowling then went to Portugal to work as an English teacher. She wanted to use her free time abroad to finish her book. But it didn't quite work out as planned. She met a man, they fell in love, and she became pregnant.

Fast forward two years later, she was a single mother, living off unemployment checks. And that's when she decided to start over with a determination that nothing would stop her this time. She used every second while the baby was sleeping to work on her book. When she had finished, she sent the manuscript to one publisher. And then another. And another. Rejection after rejection. That was the turning point. She wasn't afraid of failure anymore. She learned to embrace it. So, she kept sending manuscripts to other publishers. Twelve rejections in total. However, she used the feedback to improve the book, and she didn't lose faith. Finally, one publisher agreed to publish the book, although he was a bit skeptical. You know the rest of the story. Harry Potter became a bestseller immediately. People were begging her to write a second book. The movie soon followed, and she became a millionaire. After that, a billionaire.

Can you imagine what would have happened if she gave up after 10 rejections? The world would never have known about Harry Potter. And she would have spent the rest of her days believing that her book wasn't worthy and that she was a failure. It's funny that she once mentioned this one point when society viewed her as a failure in all areas. She was a single mother, she had no money, no job, just that silly dream of becoming a famous author. But the most important thing was that she still believed in herself and didn't give up on her goals. If you could learn only one thing from J.K. Rowling, it should be to embrace your failures. You should not see them as obstacles. Instead, look at them as chances to grow.

Why Failure Is an Essential Component of Your Success

Failure is an inevitable part of life, and there's no lasting success without failure. If someone tells you differently, it means they've been too afraid to even try and spent their lives in their own safe harbor. The sooner you learn to accept your failures, the more you will grow as a person. The most successful people in the world look forward to their failures. Because they understand that beneath every failure, there's a chance for immense growth. Below, I will give you eight reasons why failure can actually be good for you and your business. You may not be able to accept it immediately, but at least you will be open to the idea that failure isn't necessarily always something negative.

Failure Is a Reminder That You Have Tried

Too many people go through life wasting their potential because they are too afraid to try. The only people who've never failed are those who've never tried to do anything brave. I believe it's much better to try and fail than to spend years postponing your dreams. It is better to fail and learn something from it than to wonder what would have happened if you hadn't given it a go. You should be proud of all your failures because they put you in the category of brave people who aren't afraid to do something differently. It means you have all it takes to succeed, all you have to do is keep trying.

Failure Teaches Important Lessons

There are a lot of things you can learn from your failures. They don't teach this subject at school nor can you learn them through someone else's experience. Often, you have to go through failure to understand some life lessons that will help you achieve all you've ever wanted. These life experiences are much more valuable than the knowledge you can gain from business books. Failure is a much better teacher than success. It shows you what you've been doing wrong and what you can improve on.

Failure Gives You a New Perspective

When you start working on an idea, everything seems perfect, and you can't imagine any obstacles. I mean, you will think of some potential obstacles, but you can never know what will happen in the future. It's often a surprise when your idea doesn't work out because of some silly detail you never even thought about. Failure will teach you not to take anything for granted. It will help you view your idea from a different perspective. The next time, you will be ready to face more challenges than the first time, and you will already have a solution for them.

Failure Makes You More Flexible

Sometimes it's better not to get everything at the first attempt. If everything works out perfectly, you will get used to it, and you will expect it always to be like that. This approach can make you weak and unprepared for future challenges. It is much better to fail and learn to adapt to anything that may come your way. Unexpected occurrences can happen at every point of your journey. The sooner you become flexible, the easier it will be to deal with them. You will learn to transform obstacles into opportunities.

Failure Saves You from Complacency

This may sound strange, but it is true. If you are too comfortable where you are, you will refuse any change. Why would you change anything if everything works just fine? Well, this is one of the worst things that could happen to a business. You stop putting in the requisite effort, you stop innovating, and you stop dreaming. And that's the road to degradation, but the ride is so slow that you don't notice it. When a failure happens, it may turn everything upside down, but it will make you get out of your comfort zone and learn something new. You will soon realize it was one of the best things that happened to your business because you were heading in the wrong direction without knowing it.

Failure Sheds Light on Opportunities

Similar to the previous point, when you are safe in your harbor, you may be losing out on many chances and opportunities. Or maybe you don't have time to focus on opportunities along the way, so you ignore them. Failure will force you to freshly view a variety of paths and possibilities. You may remember people or problems that you were too busy to think about. One of those opportunities could change your business or your life for good.

Failure Will Show You What Really Matters

Many people describe failure as an eye-opening experience. It allows you to look at everything the way it is and not the way you want it to be. Maybe you will realize you were focusing on details too much. Maybe it will help you change your priorities and use your time and your resources in a smarter way. It could also show you that you didn't even care about that project that much. And that's also fine because you can now focus on other tasks without feeling guilty.

Failure Is Your Chance to Change

If you haven't changed anything in a long time, failure could be a blessing. You may not realize it immediately, but you will soon understand. There's no real success without change and going forward. But it's so easy to forget that. It is a natural cycle. If you don't innovate, it is inevitable to fail. However, there's nothing bad about it. Failure is your chance to reinvent yourself and your business and make everything better than it was before.

This is a rule in business, and everyone who understands it learns to be grateful for failures and obstacles on their way.

The Key Strategy – Doing What You Do Best

Success is about doing what you do best and actually enjoying it. And there's a really fabulous book about getting more done in less time. And it is an old classic in the business world. The book I am talking about is *Eat That Frog* by Brian Tracy. There's a bold statement in this book about identifying the three things that you do in your organization to bring value. This can apply to everyone, no matter whether you are a business owner, CEO, or manager. Brian Tracy states that 90% of the value you contribute to your company comes from the three things you do better than anybody else. These three talents, whatever they are, bring value, and everything else you do is a support task or complementary role. Those other tasks should not be your priorities. You can delegate or outsource them or even eliminate them. If this seems too radical to you, I really recommend reading the whole book. It's a short afternoon read, but it can help you set priorities in your life.

Doing what you do best has multiple benefits. First, it is the only way to succeed. You can't truly be successful in something you aren't excited about. Second, you will feel happier and more satisfied. And finally, it is the only way to help other people and create something that will change their lives. All entrepreneurs found that one skill they are best at and that was a turning point in their career. Warren Buffet is a genius when it comes to investing. And that's why that's the thing he focuses on. Steve Jobs was best in marketing, it was his passion. That's why once he started Apple, he didn't bother much with hardware. He left it to other people who were the best in that field. It is that simple.

If everyone focused only on a few tasks they are fantastic at, the world would be a much better place. Companies would perform better, and their employees would be much happier. If you are not sure about what your strong points are, don't worry. In the beginning, it is okay to try new things. As your business expands, you will figure out what you are naturally great at, and you can focus on that direction. You should also identify those activities that take too much time. Think about whether they are really necessary for your business. You may find interesting insights that will help you cut out all unnecessary stuff. However, if you think that you still need them, it has never been easier to delegate or outsource tasks. There are a lot of people who can do it much better and more efficiently than you, and that's normal. Remember that no one can be fantastic at everything. Therefore, the goal is to identify what you are great at and clear the deck for it.

Embrace Your Goals

There are a couple of points I'd like you to remember before the next chapter. First, it is all about identifying what you want to do and what your goals are. Goal setting is an essential process as your goals serve as a map to remind you where you are going. At the same time, identify what you do best and what you enjoy most. You should base your business on those insights. You will see that this approach has many benefits in the long run. Finally, once you determine your goals and your vision, persevere. Don't be afraid to go in the direction of your dreams, even if it means that you fail many times. There's nothing wrong with failure if you understand it. I hope this book will help you learn how to transform your failures into opportunities. Because they really are chances. They can be an opportunity to reflect on your goals and your journey to change something or completely reinvent your business. Every successful woman has faced many obstacles and many failures along the way, but they didn't let it stop them.

CHAPTER 5

Striving to Lead

"Be strong, but not rude. Be kind, but not weak. Be bold, but don't bully. Be humble, but not shy. Be confident, but not arrogant." – Jim Rohn

If I had to choose only one leader who made a difference in the twentieth century, I wouldn't choose any president or prime minister. I'd select Eleanor Roosevelt. And you may say she wasn't a president herself, only the First Lady, which also gave her a certain level of power. But I believe she was a born leader who was making a difference long before her husband became president, or even before they got married. Because leadership isn't about your title or your power. Authentic leadership is about your character, the way you treat others, and what you hold within. And she was a woman with very modern and brave ideas for that period. She wasn't afraid to speak up for herself and others, especially for vulnerable groups.

Her early life wasn't very happy. In fact, she became an orphan when she was only 10 years old. Some people would dwell on that for the rest of their lives, but she refused to feel like a victim. That was the attitude that defined her for the rest of her life. This tragic experience allowed her to understand and empathize with others. She always wanted to listen to stories of people she met throughout the country, which is why Americans loved her. She became an advocate for the rights of minorities, the disadvantaged, and the poor.

Her leadership style was authentic in so many ways. She refused to change just to meet the expectations of politicians and people in high positions. When she became First Lady, she already had a history of volunteering for different causes. She was active in the American Red Cross, and she used to volunteer in Navy hospitals. Moreover, from an early age, she was passionate about women's issues, fighting for equal opportunities. So, in her first public speech, she informed the nation not to expect their First Lady to be a symbol of elegance. She was simply Mrs. Roosevelt, who was fighting for the same causes they were.

At the time, there were still many state efforts not to allow married women to work. Eleanor wrote an outstanding newspaper column explaining her views. She insisted that women and men deserve equal opportunities for education and employment. Eleanor spent her life fighting for equal pay, economic security, and opportunities for women. She was the First Lady who organized her own press conferences. Knowing that there was still a lot of discrimination in journalism, she invited only women reporters to her conference. This gave them an exclusive opportunity to spread her story. That's a stunning example of authentic leadership. It wasn't enough to talk about equal opportunities. She went further and gave them a chance to show their qualities to the world.

Eleanor became famous for her trips throughout the country. She didn't care about state capitals, tall buildings, or the best companies. She cared about things where she could actually make a difference. Things that politicians before her ignored for decades, offering false promises and hopes. Eleanor wanted to see the working and living conditions of the poorest people living in the most far-fetched corners of the United States. Can you imagine their surprise when the First Lady appeared at their front door? She had this fantastic characteristic to leave everyone better than she found them. People admired her warmth, decency, and empathy. But she wasn't there only to give them hope. Her visit was just the first step toward change. She would then relay everything she saw to her husband, and they would work out a solution to help those people. Eleanor was like a middleman between the president and the nation. Not only because he didn't have enough time, but also because people with Eleanor's social skills and empathy were extremely rare.

She was a visionary who understood the power of movements. She knew that no matter how many people loved her, she was still an individual. And as such, she wasn't able to do a great deal. She understood the importance of building supportive communities and social movements. Eleanor joined the women's club movement and spent her whole life fighting for women's issues. She was also a member of movements fighting for improving working conditions and an activist for desegregation. After her husband's death, President Truman appointed her to the United Nations General Assembly. This was a significant milestone, but that title wouldn't mean much if the people didn't know she earned it through her hard work.

Today, many people don't understand the difference between leading and managing. Many of them have leadership positions and believe that's enough. They get to call themselves leaders. But the title is empty. Authentic leadership comes from setting an example to your employees – not from micromanaging their daily tasks. This chapter will be all about understanding this difference. It may be one of the most important things you will learn in this book, whether you are a business owner or a manager. Too many people wait until they reach a certain position in the hierarchy before they start leading. It doesn't work that way. If you wait for the next promotion, you may never become an authentic leader. Remember that it is not about titles or prestige. Your actions and your character make you a leader. People can tell who is genuine and who is not, and being an authentic leader is the best way to gain their respect.

The Eight Differences Between a Manager and a Leader

Maybe you are not sure what the difference is between a manager and a leader. And that's perfectly fine because no one talks about that. Too many people assume it is the same thing, although that couldn't be less true. This isn't an abstract book, and my goal is to give you examples from real life that you can use to help you grow. After going through this list of differences between a manager and a leader, you will have a better understanding. Then, focus on how you can implement leadership characteristics into your life and work.

Leaders Are Authentic, Managers Are Similar to Each Other

This is the core difference between a manager and a leader. Managers are sometimes afraid to embrace their uniqueness. They have to attend many training courses to teach them how to behave, and how to manage people. That's why they behave the way they think everybody expects them to. Leaders are not afraid to be different. They are not afraid to stand out and show their true self, even if it means someone will judge them. They do what they believe is right, not what business books tell them to do. To put it this way: If you meet a manager outside of work, you will discover the true personality you didn't know they had. They may be the warmest and funniest persons ever, but they are not showing it at work because they believe that's not how a manager should behave. But if you meet a leader outside of work, there'll be no surprises. They are always themselves, with all their strengths and flaws on show.

Leaders Are Innovators, Managers Maintain the Status Quo

There's a big difference between what society expects from leaders and what it expects from managers. Big companies hire good managers to help them maintain the status quo. The company has established some systems and processes that work, and now they need someone efficient to oversee them. They are not aware that there's room for improvement. That's why some mediocre companies are afraid of authentic leaders. Leaders never settle; they always want to experiment, change, and improve. Their minds see potential in everything, and it is hard to ignore that instinct. Genuine leaders strive to make the world a better place even though they know it will require some changes that may be scary at first.

Leaders Have a Vision, Managers Set Goals

Wait, didn't I just talk about the importance of goal setting? I love goals, they keep me going forward. However, there's a big difference in how you set your goals. If you set your goals because someone told you that's important, you may be going in the wrong direction. I don't suggest setting goals just for the sake of goals. Authentic leaders always see the bigger picture, and they have a vision. They know where they want to go, and goals help them to get there one step at a time. On the other hand, managers often focus too much on goals, metrics, and targets without even understanding them. They never stop to think about what the goals mean, or if there's a way to improve them. They are often working to realize someone else's vision instead of their own. Moreover, leaders are better at motivating people. They share their vision with them as well as the long-term benefits for the whole team. That's much more inspiring than setting targets and asking your people to achieve them next month without explaining them.

Leaders Focus on Relationships, Managers Focus on Rules

Leaders know that business is all about people. Whether it is their team, their clients, or business partners. Managers too often focus on rules, metrics, numbers that they forget all those aspects that wouldn't be there if it wasn't for the people. You will often hear a manager say that they don't have time to build relationships. They are too busy with their paperwork and writing reports. Leaders take time to develop meaningful relationships with other people, even if it means they won't have time for something else. People can feel when someone is genuinely interested in them. Leaders take time to listen to the needs of their employees, and they always show respect and appreciation. That's how you build loyalty and trust that can have benefits for everyone in the long run.

Leaders Create Communities, Managers Want Titles

Leaders have high self-esteem, they know their worth, so they don't need titles. They are not striving to be at the top of the hierarchy. They don't look on other people like they are subordinates, they believe they're all equal. Both managers and leaders can gain respect from their associates. But only an authentic leader can gain trust, which is priceless. There's an easy way to test whether your employees see you as a leader or a manager. If they often come to ask you for advice, they perceive you as a leader. They are not afraid to show you their vulnerability. They are not afraid to show you their imperfections, because they know you won't judge them. They know that you can work out every situation together as a team. If your people feel free to talk to you and they are not hiding anything, it means you are doing a great job as a true leader.

Leaders Are Not Afraid of Risks, Managers Hate Risk

As I already mentioned, there can be no real progress without taking risks. Leaders understand this, and they are willing to take risks. Of course, they'd never put at risk something that could have negative consequences on other employees. They are willing to take full responsibility for everything they do. It takes a lot of courage to do that. Leaders are not afraid of failures, and they see them as an opportunity to grow. But managers are so scared of risks that they will do anything to prevent them. That's because they are not able to see the bigger picture. They see only the negative sides of risks, and they are not able to see all the potential benefits. Managers and leaders have completely opposite ways of thinking.

Leaders Learn New Skills, Managers Rely on Proven Skills

Have you noticed that every training program for managers looks the same? The skills they are learning are essential to every successful person. Everyone can benefit from skills such as time management, planning, and budgeting. But once they learn those skills, managers tend to focus only on improving those specific areas. They never stop to ask themselves whether there's something more. Leaders are different. They are always learning and growing, that's in their nature. Lifetime learners! They have an unconventional approach, and they try different methods. Some of them function while others don't. But, hey, is there any other way to find out what works for you if you don't experiment?

Leaders Think Long-Term, Managers Think Short-Term

Leaders can see the bigger picture, allowing them to be more flexible in their daily activities. Let me explain. Managers tend to focus on their short-term goals. If they realize that the end of the month is approaching and their team hasn't reached the monthly goal, they will start to panic. They are afraid of what other managers might think or what their CEO will say. They don't realize that maybe their team did some other, more meaningful tasks that month. They don't realize that not reaching their goals might seem like a bad thing now, but it is actually not that bad in the long run. They will make up for it the next month. But one-time opportunities don't come that often, so it is essential to know when to be flexible and take advantage of them.

The Ten Qualities That All Great Leaders Have

Now that you are aware of the differences between a leader and a manager, we can focus on qualities that all great leaders have. Every leader is unique, and they all have an authentic leadership style. However, they all have common traits, and I believe it is necessary to develop these qualities. Therefore, I suggest you start from here and then, with time, build your own leadership style.

Honesty

Great leaders are people that others can trust. Gaining someone's trust and loyalty is one of the most challenging tasks, as it is a long process. However, it all starts with honesty and transparency. Being honest in good times is easy, especially if that's in alignment with your character. Being honest in tough times is what's hard. Honesty means you are completely transparent with your employees and your business partners. Even if you have some bad news, don't try to hide it from them. They may find out from someone else, and you will lose the respect you've been building for years. Don't worry, as people will appreciate your honesty more than they'd appreciate you sugarcoating the truth. What's more, being honest is the only way you can make your employees be honest with you. Because how could you expect something that you are not capable of giving first?

Communication

As I mentioned, business is all about creating meaningful relationships. You need to be an excellent communicator so you can share your vision with your team and motivate them. Communication skills are essential for avoiding misunderstandings and solving potential problems. And being a leader will put you in many uncomfortable situations. But that's not all bad news, because uncomfortable situations allow you to grow and become an even better communicator. If you think you lack these skills, I encourage you to start practicing them today. There are a lot of resources online. Great courses abound. But you can learn informally as well, as you can practice them every day with people you meet. You can become an exceptional communicator by practicing with your family, friends, and co-workers. It is just essential to challenge yourself and commit to improvement.

Decisiveness

As a leader, your responsibilities will grow. You will have to make important decisions involving more people. Sometimes these decisions regard only your team, other times they will impact on the whole company, or even the community. Excellent decision-making skills don't mean you will always make the best decision. No one can guarantee that. It only means that you should be able to deal with the consequences of your decision. You have to take full responsibility. Once you make a decision, there's no going back. There's no time to dwell on whether you've done the right thing. You have to get the most out of it for yourself and your team. And I believe you should not make important decisions without consulting with other stakeholders. The final word is yours, but you should also hear different opinions and appreciate new insights.

Motivation

Great leaders are not only highly motivated, but they know how to motivate others. Motivation is infectious! One of the differences between a manager and a leader is that managers give tasks to other people while leaders set an example for them. You have to learn to motivate other people. Because motivated employees are much more efficient than those just doing something because you told them to. Inspiring and motivating others is an art, but once you learn it, nothing will be able to stop you. The best way to motivate is by your example and communicating benefits. But stay away from exaggerating and false promises. Because if you do that once, you may lose the reputation that took you years to build.

Confidence

It is not possible to be a great leader if you are not self-confident. It is simple. If you doubt your own decisions, other people will doubt them as well. If you lack self-confidence and self-esteem, it is one of the first areas you should work on. Don't worry, as even the greatest leaders weren't born with all these traits. Confidence is something that you can practice and develop. Moreover, it comes with experience. Don't confuse confidence with pretending you are perfect. No one expects you to be perfect, as we all know that perfection isn't possible. Being confident doesn't mean you have to hide your flaws. Embrace them. Great leaders are not afraid of showing their weaknesses, as they make them seem more human, and people can identify with them. Know who you are and believe in yourself.

Humility

Think about the greatest leaders of all time, the ones you admire the most. They were down to earth and didn't let their success or fame change them. It is easy to start humble, but it is a real challenge to stay humble along the way. Even when you achieve all you ever wanted, don't forget where you have started from or who was there to help you. Don't forget about your own people. Real leaders are generous and selfless. They always want to help others. Make sure you let your people know you are there for them. They will appreciate you for that. And if you are fair to them, they will work

10 times harder not to disappoint you. The more you give, the more you will get. We will talk a lot about being a leader with a humble heart.

Numeracy

Don't worry if you weren't brilliant at math in school. The numeracy I am talking about doesn't have to do much with that. You don't have to be a great mathematician, but you do have to be comfortable with numbers. It is more about problem solving and developing a particular way of thinking. It is not too abstract, and actually, it is very logical. If you want to be a financial leader, you have to learn to get insights from numbers. This is something that will come to you naturally with time, but you have to practice. If you don't have this skill now, be honest with yourself. Hone it. It may be a good idea to find a financial advisor who can teach you how to develop the skill. They can instruct you via real examples until you become comfortable with numbers yourself.

Emotional Intelligence

Just like you have to learn to deal with numbers, you have to learn how to deal with people. And that is one of the biggest challenges for every leader. People can be tough, they can be shy, sometimes they won't tell you what's troubling them. If so, it is your job to find it out. And the only way you can do that is by having exceptional emotional intelligence. If this concept is new to you, I suggest you study this in a big way! Books and self-help gurus abound in this area. They can help you to better understand yourself and the people around you. This skill is precious for every leader, as it can help you solve conflicts or completely prevent them.

Results-Oriented

It is easy to idealize leaders and say that their only job is to inspire and motivate others. But as a leader, it is not all about inspiration, it must also yield results. Take for example a financial leader. When you are a financial leader, you have a lot of responsibilities. It is easy to slip into the role of motivator and forget about your targets. Your job is to find a balance between inspiring people and actually working toward your goals. Because, in the end, meeting financial goals is your responsibility. Great leaders never allow themselves to forget about their goals and why they've started. Results-oriented leadership is deadly focused on the outcome.

Resilience

Things won't always go as planned. You have to learn to pick yourself and your team up and start over. This is a key characteristic of every great leader. For employees, it is far easier. They don't have to be strong as there's always someone to watch their back and come up with a solution. Well, that someone is you. It is a tough and responsible role, but it is also a privilege. It means you are wise and strong enough to carry everyone and make sure you go forward. When the tough time comes, and nothing is working out the way it should, your employees might complain and panic. That's normal. Not everyone has all it takes to become a leader. But you should not do that. They expect you to come up with a solution. So, you should train your mind to always think in that direction. Where everyone else sees only problems, leaders see opportunities and create solutions.

Becoming Confidently Humble

When I talked about characteristics that every leader needs to develop, I mentioned they need to be confident but humble. It is not common to see those two words in the same sentence, and it is even less common to find them in one person. That's why you may feel confused, and that's fine. People with these two characteristics are very rare, but they are capable of achieving great things. They are good friends, supportive parents, fantastic colleagues, but most importantly, they are great leaders.

There's a fine line between being confident and being arrogant. Don’t worry, I am not saying you are arrogant! However, as you become more successful and achieve your goals, your self-esteem will rise. That's fantastic because confident people tend to have more success. But there's one trick to all of this. I am sure you know someone who changed profoundly after a big breakthrough. Maybe they've earned a lot of money, run a successful business, or become famous. They are no longer the person they used to be. Success made them believe they deserved more than other people. It changed the way they think about themselves and others and the way they behave. They became arrogant, and they started treating other people with disrespect.

People often believe humbleness is something bad. If you are humble, people will think you lack confidence. Moreover, others will try to make you do things you don't want to because you don't know how to say no. Well, that's not what humility is about. Humility is a trait that keeps you down to earth even if you become a millionaire. It is good because it doesn't allow you to lose touch with reality. The most successful people are humble. They treat other people with respect, and that's why everyone likes to be around them. Therefore, your goal should be to increase your confidence but to stay humble. That's why I like to say you should be confidently humble. It sums everything up perfectly. If this sounds too abstract, don't worry. I will give you some practical tips on implementing this principle in your daily life.

Be Open to Receive Feedback

When we're new to a field, we're open to feedback and appreciate it. Do you remember your first business mentors? Their tips and feedback probably helped you grow and become the professional you are today. As they become experts in some field, people don't listen to the feedback of others that much. And that's the biggest mistake you can make. Not only will feedback help you stay down to earth, but it can also help you improve. If you ignore other people's feedback, you may miss chances to grow and improve yourself. Therefore, always ask your colleagues and clients for feedback, and be open to their opinions.

Practice Gratitude

Gratitude can transform your life in many ways. With regards to business, it can help you appreciate how far you've come, but without arrogance. Practicing gratitude will teach you not to take things for granted, and it will make you humbler. If you don't know where to start, here's what you can do. Each night before you go to sleep, think about three good things that happened that day. Three items you are grateful for. You can also use gratitude to improve your relationships with other people and show them you appreciate them. Gratitude isn't just about saying thank you when someone does you a favor. It is about reminding people that they are important to you and that they are doing a great job. I encourage you to try doing this, and you will surely see fantastic results.

Make a List of Your Strengths and Flaws

Both lists are equally important, as they help you reach a balance. If you struggle with self-confidence, make a list of your strengths and all your accomplishments. Keep it as a reminder of how far you've come when you feel down. Alternatively, a list of your flaws has additional benefits. If you become too concerned with your wins, you should keep this list as a reminder that no one is perfect. Before you judge your co-workers, this list can remind you that we're all human and that we all have our flaws. There's one more thing. You can use this list as a guide to remind you what areas you still have to work on. There's always room for improvement. Lifetime learning... wink!

Be Kind

People often underestimate the power of kindness. You can recognize a true leader by the way they treat those above them. Genuine leaders treat everyone with respect and kindness. No matter if your day was stressful, there's no reason to treat other people badly. And by other people, I mean everyone – your family, your colleagues, or those cleaning your office. If you behave rudely or arrogantly, people may only act as if they respect you. They are often just too afraid to show disrespect. But the only way to gain someone's genuine respect is by treating them with kindness and compassion. To be honest, showing kindness helps you far more than the recipient. It is one of those things that brings great joy in giving.

Try New Things

For many experts, it is easy to slip into arrogance and complacency when they become the best at what they do. There's no competition around them, so it can be almost natural to think you are somehow superior. I have a quick recipe to change your mindset. You should remind yourself what it feels like to be a beginner. Naturally, you can't become a beginner in your field, but you can become a beginner in anything else. It doesn't even have to be anything business-related. You can try a new sport, a new craft, a new skill. At least for a day, to see how it feels when you are a beginner.

When you return to your office, you may be even more confident in your skills, but your worldview will be different.

Leadership – A Rare but Valuable Trait

I find it very challenging to describe leadership. As you can see, it is not one skill or characteristic. It is actually a set of characteristics that a good leader needs to have. You may have some of them naturally, but you may need to practice others. Leadership is a beautiful tapestry of natural ability and a desire to continually build on your talent. Influencing others is challenging and rewarding. It is something that you have to experience first-hand. Remember, managers go to training programs and learn how to manage people and measure success. Leadership is something more profound than that. It may take years to become a great leader and to gain people's trust. But don't let that discourage you, as it is absolutely worth it. Start today. Work on your mindset. Convince yourself that you have all it takes to become an excellent leader in your field or your company. See what characteristics you already have and compliment yourself on them. Then, see what traits you lack, and make a plan on how you can practice and improve these skills. Remember, practice makes perfect, and that's true for leaders as well.

CHAPTER 6

Balancing Work & Life

"Joy is the happiness that doesn't depend on what happens." – David Steindl-Rast

I recently moved to a new neighborhood where my landscaper could no longer cut my grass. Clearly, it was time to find a new landscaper. I am a single mother and a busy professional woman. I think the expectation is that I will always have someone hired to do this. No one would expect me doing it myself. Initially, a friend came over, and he cut my grass. I was inside watching and thinking about how much I love mowing a lawn.

I remember doing it with my dad when I was a little girl. I like the smell of cut grass, and I like how it all looks so perfect afterward. I simply enjoy it, and I take pride in it. In the end, I never hired a new landscaper. I decided to do it myself. Ladies, it burns about 300 calories and takes 3,000 steps to cut my grass. I absolutely track that stuff and spend money to achieve it. So, why not go outside and mow my yard? It turned out I liked it so much, I didn't want to stop doing it. Helpful neighbors tried to give me numbers of their landscapers, but I said: "No, thank you." I love being outside. I love my yard. It relaxes me and makes me feel good. On the other hand, I'd rather walk off the plank of a pirate ship than mop and vacuum my floors and scrub my bathroom. And that's okay. I made the decision to personally take care of the yard and hire a housekeeper. I learned that the only way to achieve a work/life balance is to delegate the tasks I don't enjoy doing. It allows me to concentrate on my strengths and to be more efficient and happier.

Don't Try and Do Everything Yourself

One of the most common mistakes when starting your own business is trying to do everything yourself. We've all been there, and I think it is especially common for women because we're used to multitasking. But the good news is we don't have to! This may be a shock to you, but trying to do everything yourself, in business or in life, is a recipe for disaster. Even if you are great at all those tasks, you simply don't have time for everything. It will lead you to burn out, and you will eventually have to take a break. Life is all about setting priorities. Focus only on what you like or something that only you can do and delegate everything else. This can apply to all areas of life – cooking, cleaning, or hiring a personal assistant to deal with your documents. Below, I will share a list of reasons why delegating can be so beneficial.

Teamwork Is Better Than Individual Work

When you are working alone, you can do only a limited number of tasks as there are only 24 hours in a day. When you have a great team, you can delegate and outsource work, and together you can accomplish much more in the same 24 hours. Even the most successful individuals have their teams behind them. Maybe you don't get to see them, but they are there, doing their part of the job. It is like in sports. Michael Jordan is a fantastic player, but if he were playing alone against the other team, he'd inevitably lose. Even though he might be a better player than any other individual player in the other team. As a group, they are stronger together. Therefore, your goal should be to create a team of highly-skilled people you can trust. Creating and managing teams is a skill worth learning. We will talk about it later in more detail.

Two Heads Are Better Than One

No one can be an expert in every field. Even if you spend your whole life learning, there will always be something you don't know. And that's perfectly fine. The best way to increase your capacities is to start collaborating with people who are experts in different fields. That way, you will have access to more knowledge and more skill than any one individual. There's nothing wrong with learning from your colleagues or even your subordinates. I will paraphrase Henry Ford who said that the best skill he had was the ability to surround himself with people who were experts in different fields. He didn't need to know anything about mechanics. But he knew who he had to call, and that person would be able to solve a problem much faster and better than Ford himself. And he was okay with that because he knew that's the only way to succeed. Henry Ford didn't invent outsourcing, but he made that concept popular by talking about it openly. You have to admit that you can't do it all, and you have to find the right people to help you.

Nobody Has Done Anything Big Alone

Think about everything great humankind has created. Nobody has ever done anything that changes the world alone. Architectural wonders, the Industrial Revolution, big discoveries, or even successful startups. No one was alone. Help can come in numerous shapes and forms. It doesn't always have to be your business partner. Sometimes, it is a supportive family member, your mentor, teacher, or someone who likes your project and wants to give financial support. Maybe it is a nanny who takes care of your kids so you can go to that important meeting that can change the course of your business. Everyone needs someone to help them, at least a little. History tends to remember only those who became famous in the process. It tends to forget that there were numerous other people and that without their work, that individual wouldn't have been able to go very far.

Don't let success stories fool you that they accomplished everything alone and that you should do the same.

Delegation is King

I am a big fan of delegating. When I started doing so, I freed up so much time for the activities that really matter. And I became more productive because I was finally able to concentrate on the more important matters. Here are some great reasons to delegate and the benefits you can reap.

You Will Have Time to Focus on Things You Do Great

If you are desperately trying to do everything alone, your business may actually be suffering. You are giving yourself too many tasks to do, which doesn't leave you enough time to focus on tasks that matter. Do you really have to spend hours every day entering data into spreadsheets? Is there anyone else who can do it? When you delegate simple, ordinary tasks, you will finally have time to focus on the tasks you do better than anyone else in the world. Maybe you are great at creating strategies or brainstorming. The world needs to hear your ideas. Don't waste your precious time doing mundane things when you could be designing and implementing new ideas in your business. I believe everyone should do only what they do best. If you are fantastic at the creative part but terrible at accounting, don't worry, there's someone whose dream job is to become an accountant. And delegating tasks can be a win-win situation for both of you.

Together You Can Get More Things Done

As I said, we only have 24 hours in a day. But when we share our duties with someone, we can easily multiply the number of hours we have. You will know that your business is growing when you start to experience so-called bottlenecks. It is a situation when everything and everyone is waiting, and they can't proceed with their operations because something is being held up. This is a good sign, although it doesn't look like it. It means your business is expanding, otherwise you wouldn't have that much work to do, right?

It may be time to hire someone to help you handle everything. This will increase the efficiency and productivity of your business. As a result, your business will grow instead of stagnating because you can't do everything on time. Accordingly, you will have to expand your team and hire more people. Doesn't this sound fantastic? Something that started as an idea in your mind now gives work to many people. You should be proud of yourself. You cannot lead while others grow... unless you delegate.

Empowering Your Employees

People quickly lose motivation if you ask them to repeat the same things over and over again. You can prevent this if you allow them to learn and grow by occasionally challenging them with new tasks. This can be beneficial for everyone involved. You are training your employees, teaching them new skills. As a result, they are becoming more and more capable so you can rely on them fully. This is important in everyday situations because it boosts productivity at all levels. But you will especially see the benefits of training your employees if you are ever away. Let's say you have a business trip or a family problem that requires you to be absent from work. This is a big test both for you and your employees. If you've been handling almost everything alone, you have the right to panic because your employees may not be capable of working without you. But if you've trained your staff, you can leave for a couple of days, safe in the knowledge that everything will be fine when you return. As you can see, by delegating, you are actually giving yourself more freedom to take a break when you need it. And you will surely need it, although it may not look like that to you now.

Achieving Work/Life Balance

"Balance is not something you find, it is something you create." – Jana Kingsford

Everyone is talking about work/life balance, but what does that actually mean? It is not an abstract concept. In fact, it is something that should be normal, but we tend to forget that because we work too much. For many people, their work is the most important part of their life, although it should be just one of the areas. Work/life balance means having an equilibrium between your professional life, personal life, family life, social life, or any other area that may be important to you. Whether it is sport, wellness, spiritual life, or some hobby. It is essential to find balance in everything you do.

Work/life balance is one of my very favorite topics. I think, as women, it is probably one of the most significant issues in our lives. I believe that, by design, we have a little more complexity in our personal needs and desires. And I can't say enough about how developing your own work/life balance can change your world. So, let's just be clear. Forget all this talk about some people just doing it better than others. None of this talk of "I am a victim", and "I can't achieve a work/life balance". Creating balance is something you deliberately do. There are many books and podcasts that can explain this concept much better than I can. But I can share some things I am very passionate about and that work in my life. One of them is that planning your ideal year, or your ideal month, or your ideal week, or even your ideal day, is absolutely essential. It is not always going to happen as you planned, but you have to know where your goal is. I'd suggest starting with non-negotiables in your life. Things like: "I go to church every Sunday." Or, "Little Johnny practices ball on Tuesday and Thursday afternoons." If your non-negotiable is a date night with your husband and a yoga class on

Saturdays, stick to it. That's what brings balance to your life. Once you determine your non-negotiables, look at the rest of the time you have and maximize it. Don't feel guilty about setting boundaries because we all need them. I sincerely believe in flexibility in life, but this planning principle helped me gain that balance. I will now give you some practical tips on work/life balance that function well for me.

Turn Off Your Phone

Whether you want to admit it or not, we're all addicted to our phones. Some people more than others, but, generally, we spend way more time on our phones than we should. Mobile phones are blurring the line between professional and private life. When did it become normal to receive work-related emails at 10 PM? I am talking from my personal experience as a business owner. It is so hard to set boundaries. But sometimes you have to do so for the sake of your mental health. I will share some of the tactics that worked for me so you can find something that fits in with your lifestyle. Your work emails mustn't be the first thing you read in the morning. I know you are in a hurry, and you want to read them on the go. However, you should dedicate at least 10 minutes to yourself to sit in silence and reflect on your goals for that day. Without distractions. Also, you should not be checking whether you have a new email or a new notification every 15 minutes. How can you focus on any task if you are always waiting for something on your phone? Instead, you should schedule some time in your day to answer emails. I have to do that multiple times a day, but at least I control when. I know that I am answering my emails three times a day. For the rest of the time, I try to minimize using my phone. I won't lie, it is often difficult. But it is also very energizing, and it helps me to focus on my priorities.

Make Time for Exercising

We all know that exercising is beneficial for our bodies, but it is also great for your mind. When you set some time to work out, you know you are reserving time for yourself, and no one can disturb you. Exercising is a great way to get rid of the stress that accumulates during long working days. Don't get me wrong. This isn't a fitness book, and I don't want to challenge you to become a professional athlete. No. For me, exercise is something I do in order to unwind and feel better. It can be anything, really. There's no need to go to the gym if you don't want to. I often do a couple of quick movements in my office to stretch my neck and shoulders. I encourage you to do the same, especially if you have to sit in front of your computer a lot, like me. Another great form of exercise is walking. A simple walk around the block can do wonders for your mind and productivity. But the point I want to make is that you have to schedule some time for exercising. When you don't schedule something, other matters become your priority. There's always something urgent that needs your attention, so you constantly put off exercising. Deliberately set some time to stay fit and take care of yourself. If you don't have time during the week, it can be the weekend as well. In either case, make sure you spend time outside, in nature. Sunshine is good for the soul.

Draw Boundaries

You have to set boundaries for anything that wastes your time and drains your energy. It could be some TV show, an irritating colleague, or your high school friends. Other people have to understand that you have different priorities now. It can be hard, so you have to set clear boundaries and don't give up on them. At work, it means you will finish your tasks before helping someone else. You know those people who always ask for help so you end up doing their work for them, and, as a result, leaving your own tasks behind. In your private life, it could be anyone pulling you away from your goals. For example, you want to go to a course that's important to you, professionally or as a hobby. If your friends ask you to go out just before your class starts, a person with clear boundaries will say "no" without feeling guilty. We have a whole discussion coming up about that magic word "no". You should not feel guilty for putting your needs first and being accountable to yourself.

Forget About Perfectionism

I see a lot of women struggling with perfectionism. We believe society expects us to manage everything perfectly: work, meetings, home, and on top of that, to always look flawless and never get tired. I don't say you can't have it all because I believe you can. However, you simply can't be perfect in every department. Perfectionism is stealing your time and joy. Therefore, I believe it is better to be efficient and get things done the best you can. Your best doesn't have to be perfect. You have to realize that the world isn't expecting perfection from you. We're often the ones who put all that pressure on ourselves. When it comes to working, set the time you have to do some tasks. Do your best and give 100%. But when the time's up, finish it. Send that report. Press that button. Don't waste your precious time dwelling on details that don't make any difference. Use that time to work on other areas that are important to you – your health, your family, your passions.

It Is All about Joy!

I want you to know that finding joy in your business and financial life is doable. Read over that again if it seems too good to be true. Because the one thing we probably feel like we don't have a lot of control over is our financial and business life. It is something volatile. It is something risky. It is the thing that changes due to circumstances that we can't always control. I know a lot of times we feel like we're letting the tail wag the dog in some of our decisions. So, let's think about that sentence where I boldly stated that we could find joy in our business and financial lives.

And please focus on that word "joy" for a minute. Joy isn't the same as happiness. Happiness is finding yourself in really extraordinary circumstances. I am happy when all my kids are home for Christmas. I am happy when I am at the pool in the sunshine. I am happy when I've paired the perfect wine with dinner. But that's not joy. And when it rains at that pool, I am not happy. Joy is actually being confident and at peace with what you are doing. It means that the circumstances around you can change for the better or the worse, but you don't ride that roller coaster. You don't let it affect you. Joy is a bigger picture. It is knowing that, at the end of the day, you've run things through the lens of what you really want in life. And it passes. I want us to talk about the different facets that come together in our lives, like a giant spider's web. We can't separate them from each other. We can't have a marketing discussion without talking about the work/life balance. We can't make money without talking about investing in all these areas, financial or non-financial, of this big melting pot that we call our life.

Creating lasting joy will require you to say no. We can't have it all. And I appreciate that you naturally know what you want and what you don't. Saying no to something that isn't your true passion can be so liberating. It leaves you a lot of time to focus on what you really want to grow in your life or your business. Success in business comes from determining what's worthy of your attention, and then focusing only on them. And letting the rest go. It is not something I've come up with. It is a proven principle that some of the most successful people ever used.

The Most Powerful Word in the English Language

When they asked Warren Buffet what the secret to his success was, and what did he do that other people didn't, his response was shocking. He said it wasn't about what he did, but rather about what he didn't do. Warren Buffet was a young entrepreneur when he learned an important lesson that I believe we all should learn. He realized that it is okay to say no. No to everything that doesn't fit into the big picture! It is fascinating that he focused only on a limited number of things during his career. He didn't waste his precious time focusing on unimportant stuff. He didn't let anything distract him from his goals. And don't let this fool you. It is not easy. It is way more challenging than it seems, but it is the only recipe for long-term success and achieving your goals. For Steve Jobs, it was the same. He admits he had to say no to some fantastic ideas. Because once he started working on something, hundreds of other ideas were distracting him. Maybe they were great. Maybe they were even better than his original vision. But if he had to focus on each one of them, he'd never have achieved anything. What you can learn from him is that you should be very selective in your life. But once you choose something, stick to it. Make it work. Don't give up on something you've chosen just because there's something else that seems more enticing at the moment.

Here are some of the most common things successful people say no to. You don't have to give up on all of them. But maybe this list can help you realize what's stealing the time and energy in your life.

- Successful people say no to people-pleasing. They will never do something they don't want to do just to make someone else feel better. They understand no one can benefit from that. Don't give up on your priorities just because you believe someone expects you to do something.

- Successful people say no to ideas that don't inspire them. Just because someone proposed something, it doesn't mean you have to accept it. We all have limited amount of resources – our time, our focus, and we should be really careful about how we spend them. You don't have to accept ideas that are not in alignment with your values, your vision, or that just don't bring you joy. Be polite, say thank you, but politely refuse those ideas.

- Successful people say no to energy vampires. I am sure you have these people around you. Maybe some of your friends or your colleagues. You should not spend time with people who drag you down. You don't need that kind of negativity in your life. It is one of the best things you can do for your mental wellbeing.

- Successful people say no to working overtime. Of course, when you run your own business, there are times it seems that you work constantly. Consistently and routinely working very long hours is not an optimal lifestyle. It will lead you to stress, burnout, and it can even cause health problems. It can affect relationships with your loved ones because it depletes quality time together.

- Successful people say no to events they don't feel like attending. For example, just because someone invited you to that networking event, it doesn't mean you have to go. Especially if you've planned something else for that evening. Networking events are not the only way to build business relationships. There are many other ways, and it is important to do what feels right for you.

Balance Is Our Solution

Work is essential, but your wellbeing is even more important. If you are just starting your business, you probably feel like you have to do everything alone. I understand. I have lived it. But if you keep that hectic pace up for too long, you risk burning out. And that's something we want to avoid at all costs. The sooner you realize you are not alone, the easier everything will be for you. There's nothing wrong with delegating tasks that you can't do, or that you simply don't enjoy doing. It is a win-win situation for you and for the person who gets to do it. Because there's always someone who enjoys something you hate. Just like how I love mowing my lawn and hate cleaning my house. That's okay. We're all different. If other people want to help you, accept their help without feeling guilty. Only then can you achieve a work/life balance, which should be your ultimate goal. Maybe you won't find it immediately, but keep trying and making progress. Keep experimenting to see what habits and routines work best for you. You will know you've found it when you start waking up energized and ready to work on your dream projects.

CHAPTER 7

Women Outsell & Out-Serve

"She believed she could, so she did." – R.S. Grey

Have you ever been a waitress? No other experience, except for maybe serving in the military, draws my eye to a resume more. Waitresses, those who do well, have a variety of talents. They develop patience, an accommodating spirit, accuracy, and excellent conversational skills. They need to have a great memory and pay attention to detail. They become good listeners. They remain calm when busy and find something to do when the day is slow. They know how to deal with unhappy patrons and accept criticism. They have an incredible amount of stamina. They know how to hide their mood and smile when they don't feel like it. They understand how to marry two things that are critical in business: to have a servant's heart and add a touch of hustle for the almighty dollar.

I was a waitress in my high school and early college days. I was fortunate to work in many situations, from a country-cooking, family restaurant to an ice cream parlor, to an officers' club at a local base. In every situation, I learned so much about what it takes to be successful, to earn money, and to feel good about what you do. Let me give you an example. You are looking forward to the weekend because Saturday is your day off. Your manager asks you if you could work instead. Do you want the morning shift or the evening shift? Both please!

Let me tell you, there's something in your heart when you need the money and you are willing to work that makes you want to get there early and stay late. Accordingly, you arrive early to get the best tables assigned to you. The ones you know that turn quickly, that are easy to work with, and that make you the most money. In the meantime, you put on your most comfortable shoes because you know that you are going to be on your feet for 14 hours. You are not going to stop, sit down, or take a break. And you are going to leave with more money than most people like you make in a week. But in doing so, you’ve also smiled and talked to people from all walks of life. And you've impacted them for an hour or two during that day. You share stories, and laugh, and you connect with people. You could have a great day and feel good about what you do while making money. Every time I see that listed in somebody's background, I think: This is a person I want on my team.

Marketing and Selling Success Isn't About Tracking

Let's talk about marketing and selling for a moment. Now, I am no marketing guru. And many leaders in the world can give you all kinds of technical skill sets and tools that can enhance your ability to market and sell. However, in this book, I want to talk about the spirit of the process. I want to talk about your actual motivations for marketing and selling and show how important and impactful they are. If you want an excellent read on this, I suggest *Selling with Noble Purpose* by Lisa Earle McLeod. She explains how much more successful a person is when they are motivated by bringing value to their customer and helping them find a solution. I know this sounds clichéd, like a super warm and fuzzy way to sell, but it is actually grounded in truth. It lays out an excellent argument for the fact that if you motivate your people with numbers and closings, that's what they are going to look for.

You get what you incentivize. You get the culture of your business, and it reflects on everything. It reflects on the way we talk about our potential clients, how we track progress, and it defines our key performance indicators. The enlightening part of this is that people who want to help their customers are genuinely motivated. It turns out that people who sell with a noble purpose have better sales results. Numerous studies prove this, and I think it makes sense.

Why Are Women Better at Serving Customers?

Have you noticed that more women than men work in customer-oriented industries? You might think it is a coincidence, but business owners have a good reason for hiring women. The truth is that everyone can learn some customer service skills, but not all of them. What I mean is that you can't learn to show empathy if you don't have it within you. You are either born with it or not. The good news is that women are born with skills that help them become excellent at dealing with customers. I am not talking about rare characteristics here. I am talking about showing genuine interest and empathy – traits that no one can fake. Below, I've selected five natural characteristics that women have that allow us to shine in the customer-oriented world.

Women Show More Empathy

If you've ever worked in the retail industry, you know that managers expect you to empathize with unsatisfied customers. It is no longer enough to say you are sorry, the staff has to go one step beyond. You may get training courses teaching you how to act when something disappointing happens. But let's be honest. Could you pretend to be sorry when all you can think about is leaving early? That's it. You are either born with empathy or you aren't. Faking it can be counterproductive as people can sense it. Women are not only more often born with a high level of empathy, but they also get to develop it throughout childhood. Just compare the way girls talk to each other to the way boys do. Girls are always encouraging and complementing one another, while boys often don't think about those things. When your friend was heartbroken, you were with her, not because you had to but because you wanted to. You felt all that she was going through, and chances are you will feel the same way for some of your customers. Of course, exaggerating with empathy isn't a solution either. Your goal should be to find the right balance to the mutual satisfaction of you and your customers.

Women Love to Talk

Most women I know talk far more than their husbands. Now, someone may say this is a stereotype, and I am okay with it. But there's another element to this that no one will disagree with. Women are better at explaining things. Let's consider a man and woman describing a new product they've bought. Men will be concise and may relay all the details, but they often lack enthusiasm when describing things. Women, on the other hand, will not only go into detail, but they will also make you feel as if you were there. We have this power to transform emotions and involve others in our story when we talk. I think we're much better with words.

Women Are More Patient

Working with customers requires explaining the same thing over and over again. With every new call, it is like you've never talked about that topic before. And you haven't. To that specific person. For them, everything is still new, and you have to understand that and accept it. Yes, it can be repetitive, but women are more patient than men. If you are a mother, you know what I am talking about. Nature trains you to patiently respond to hundreds of questions your toddler has every single day. If you can handle your baby, believe me, you can handle any customers you want. We have our biology to thank. And we could also thank our kids and nieces and nephews that trained us to be patient. People need patience in large doses. Win for the ladies!

Women Are Problem Solvers

When we really want to solve something, no matter what that might be, we persist. We never give up, even when it seems there's no way we're going to succeed. Men are like this in some situations when they really care about something, but not always. Generally, they are more laid-back, and they will just give up and go and do something more productive. On the other hand, we persist and try various approaches until we find the one that works. Have you ever watched women shopping? When they believe they deserve a discount or they want to return an item, they will fight no matter what. If we have to talk to the manager, we'd gladly do so. This is the approach you need in business as well. The attitude that says you are not giving up until you work out a solution. Your clients and your customers will appreciate it.

Women Have More Experience in Phone Calls

It is no wonder customer support is full of females. It is as if we were born to solve our problems over the phone. Your father, brother, husband probably isn't like that. And if they can't stand solving minor family issues on the phone, how do you think they can solve angry customers using the same phone? If you've ever worked in the call center, you know it is one of the most challenging roles. You may not be aware of it, but that experience can help you deal with clients from all walks of life. Virtually, or in real life, it doesn't matter. It is safe to assume that customer service jobs are the school of life. You learn some important skills you'd never learn if you only communicated with your loved ones.

Why Are Women Better Marketers?

It is official! We now have proof that women are better marketers than men. And no, that's not something I've made up just to brighten your day. There's science behind it. What's more, the list I am going to share with you comes from a man, not a woman. Therefore, we know the list is objective. I am talking about Mark Ritson, brand consultant, and former marketing professor. Here are the seven science-based traits he believes make women better marketers.

Articulate

Male and female brains have different ways of viewing the world. Generally speaking, men tend to think systematically while women have a more holistic approach. That allows us to see the bigger picture and understand the potential consequences of our actions. While men sometimes struggle to describe their visions verbally, women don't have this problem. They are much better at articulating the world around them. We can explain our visions with more clarity to anyone willing to listen. This trait is essential for success in digital marketing, especially creative parts of it. For example, in storytelling, which is becoming more popular every day.

Attention to Detail

It would be enough to compare the way men and women dress or decorate their houses to tell who pays more attention to detail. However, I don't want to risk being superficial as there are exceptions to every rule. I will talk about marketing and brand management. Men can make a strategy to promote a brand, but women are those who come up with details that make it stand out. Without a woman's final touch, most products would look like similar copies of each other. Especially when we're talking about industries where aesthetics is important, such as fashion or design. Walk into a bachelor's home. Enough said.

Attuned

Both in personal life and in business, women tend to surround themselves with supportive communities. Successful men often see each other as competitors. Women are wiser, and they understand that they are stronger together when they combine their talents. That was probably the only way to achieve success in the past, when it was much more challenging to be a woman than now. The habit stuck with us, and I think it is very beautiful and useful. Women tend to be in harmony with other women in the market. We understand the art of collaboration.

All Heart

Women often find it challenging to separate emotions from the rational, decision-making part of our mind. But the good news is, you don't have to get rid of your feelings. Our empathy and social intelligence can help us win in business. The first task of a good marketer is to understand how its target audience feels. What do they want? What do they need? What irritates them? What triggers them? Only then can you create a successful strategy that will help you achieve the results you want.

Altruistic

Throughout history, women were responsible for caring about children and old or weak members of society. That altruistic spirit still follows us today. Why not use it to your advantage in business? Your altruistic mind can help you develop genuine benefits for your clients and create a win-win situation. Moreover, men marketers like to exhibit themselves even when they don't have anything brilliant to say. Women are more patient and wait until they really have something impressive to share with the world.

Analytical

One of the common misconceptions is that men are better with logic and numbers than women. Even though they may be faster when analyzing their results or performance, they lack some crucial skills. They don't have the holistic approach of women, and that's why they often neglect details or fail to see the bigger picture. It is safe to say our analytical results may be slower, but they are more accurate. Don't forget that it is never about quantity. It is always about quality and the good work you produce.

Age Better

Research has shown that some parts of women's brains age slower than men's. For example, men tend to become more impulsive over time. Their ability to control their emotional responses gradually decreases. It doesn't mean they are rude, they are just unaware of it. That's why, for many, their behavior changes, and it seems like they've become a different person. If we take good care of our health, women can prevent most of these issues, keeping our brain happier and healthier, no matter our age.

Get the Most Out of Your Advantages

Women are capable of everything and have hidden powers that we just need to tap into. It has never been a better time to be a woman in business and marketing than today. But what's even crazier, I believe, the best is yet to come! We're finally becoming aware of our potential, and the world is ready for a new generation of successful businesswomen. Even if you believed you had some flaws before reading this book, I hope you now know you can transform them to your advantage. The business world finally realizes the power behind things that were labeled as too girly before. I am talking about emotional intelligence, empathy, and a willingness to show your imperfections. I've got a profound message for those of you who are new to the business world and think you lack some skills. Just remember all the roles you've covered in your life – from mother and sister to waitress or babysitter when you were a teen. Those experiences are precious, as they taught you much more than you know!

CHAPTER 8

Financial Intelligence & Building Wealth

"It is not about how much money you make, but how much money you keep, how hard it works for you, and how many generations you can keep it for." – Robert Kiyosaki

I really love a concept I first read in a story called "What You Feed, Grows". One young boy talked to his grandfather, who told him that two wolves were fighting within each one of us. A good and a bad wolf. The good wolf was carrying happiness, joy, generosity, fulfillment. The bad one was carrying anger, sorrow, regret. When the young boy asked his grandfather which wolf would win, the old man simply said: "The one you feed." You can feed each of the two wolves with your thoughts, your habits, behaviors, people you spend time with, and so on. It is really up to you. You can feed each side of your personality, but what you focus on will grow and expand within you.

The same is true for your financial life. You can feed the good wolf with financial knowledge, or you can feed the bad wolf with ignorance. We often get information from the wrong resources – media, magazines, conversations with friends. But we think we're still young, and there will always be time to start organizing our finances. Are you asking about when you should start financial planning? The answer is always now, without exception. Even if you are a very inexperienced or a young reader, taking in some core education will lay out basic truths about your financial life. I would suggest reading the work of Dave Ramsey from the Financial Peace University. He's a master of explaining how to build a strong financial life. He suggests combining living frugally, establishing discipline, savings, giving, and reducing your debts.

The Real Meaning of Wealth

Nowadays, there are so many financial coaches, and each of them has their own definition of wealth. Wealth can represent different things for different people. There are some important cultural differences to consider as well. However, most experts believe your wealth is defined as your "net worth". There's a simple formula to estimate your net worth. It simply says your wealth is equal to your assets minus liabilities. Your net worth is what you own, less what you owe. Wealth is more than your money, but people generally identify wealth with their financial assets. It is such a widespread definition that it is hard to dispute it.

People sometimes use prosperity and wealth as synonyms, but that's not quite correct. Prosperity is a broader term than wealth. Actually, your financial wealth is just one part of your prosperity. Other parts include your health, wellbeing, happiness. We all know someone who is extremely wealthy but very unhappy. Whatever the cause of their condition, we can't say that this person is truly prosperous. Not if some of the areas of their life are not functioning the way they should be.

Finally, abundance. More than anything else, abundance is a state of mind. It can refer to anything, not only financial resources. You get to choose whether you observe the world from an abundance perspective or a scarcity perspective. I always suggest abundance, as I sincerely believe there are enough resources for everyone. I am not talking only about financial resources, although they are very important. I believe in the abundance of opportunities in life. I've met some affluent families who have built wealth during the decades, but they weren't able to enjoy it. They weren't able to get rid of that scarcity mindset that prevented them from relaxing. You should work both on your material wealth as well as your inner abundance.

Don’t believe anyone who tells you that you have to choose between the two and that you can’t have both.

What Is Your Money Personality?

I hope this chapter has already made you think about the relationship you have with money in your life. Even if you are not on excellent terms, it doesn't matter; what's important is that you are aware of it. There's one fun test that can tell you what your money personality is, and it is also pretty accurate. As you are reading the descriptions, try to think about which group you fit.

Spender

If one of the greatest pleasures in life is when you buy something brand-new for you or a loved one, guess what, you are a spender. It doesn't necessarily have to be something bad. However, it may be an excellent moment to think about your financial habits. You are probably not saving enough money, and you may be telling yourself that you simply don't have enough. But is that really true? You don't have to answer me. It is enough to respond to yourself: whether you can't save money or you are simply not in the habit of saving.

Amasser

The amasser is completely opposite to the spender. You like saving and investing money. Even if you earn enough, you don't feel comfortable spending too much. That's fine, as you should always be sensible. However, it may be worth it to think about your financial beliefs. Maybe deep within yourself, you fear you will lose all your security if you lose your money. There is a spirit of scarcity present. This is something to work on, alone, or with your financial coach.

Avoider

Are you always waiting until the last moment before you pay your bills or taxes? Do you even know what your monthly budget is, or do you prefer not to think about it? Maybe money makes you uncomfortable and overwhelmed because you are not used to budgeting. Maybe you are avoiding something even bigger than that. It is time you took your financial life into your own hands. I'd suggest keeping a financial journal so you can get better control of your finances.

Hoarder

Saving money is fine as long as it doesn't affect your daily life. I know a lot of hoarders who don't want to buy anything. Nothing seems valuable to them, and they'd rather keep their money. Maybe you are too serious about the idea of saving for the rainy days and need to take a more relaxed approach to your finances. If nothing else, you could consider investing your money so that it can work for you.

Money Monk

You may be one of those people who go through life believing that money is dirty. In turn, you think all wealthy people are somehow bad. The consequences can be even worse. You could start avoiding every opportunity that could help you change your financial status. You have some limiting beliefs and think you don't deserve money, or that money could make you greedy or a bad person. I encourage you to accept yourself the way you are and then change these limiting beliefs.

How to Build Your Business Acumen

Have you ever heard about business acumen? It is one of the most important aspects of business, and you should focus on building yours. Business acumen isn't one particular skill. I'd rather say it is a set of skills and knowledge that help you grow in business. Some of the most important skills include financial knowledge, understanding metrics, and strategies. They will allow you not only to understand your business better but also to set smarter goals and make better decisions. If you are new to the business world, don't worry. Business acumen isn't something you develop overnight. Experience plays a vital role in building your acumen. But there's one more thing: spending time with people who know more than you. Even the most successful business people have their mentors. Surround yourself with people who know more about finances and strategies than you do. And never shy away from asking questions.

Financial statements are one of the most challenging documents to understand, but they are vital for success. Find a mentor you can trust and let them walk you through your company's statements, step by step. You don't have to understand everything at first, but it is essential to learn to recognize the most important metrics. Another way to build your business acumen is by reading books and business news, especially those relevant to your industry. If you don't know where to start, I suggest Forbes or the Wall Street Journal. They might seem too general, but it is essential to understand the market and the bigger picture.

It is Time to Raise Your Financial IQ

In previous chapters, I've talked a lot about the importance of different types of intelligence. One of the areas I focused on the most was emotional intelligence. Now, I want to talk about one other form of intelligence that's essential for success in business: financial intelligence. And the good news is that you don't have to be born with it. Unlike your IQ, financial intelligence is something that you can learn and practice. There's no successful person who hasn't worked on their financial IQ. Simply put, this skill helps you understand your finances. And with better understanding, you will be able to make better financial decisions. You will learn how to use your resources to generate wealth. Even if you don't have many resources, know that, with good management, you can transform your financial situation faster than you think. There are a lot of reasons to work on improving your financial IQ. Below, I will give you a list of those that motivated me most.

Changing Your Financial Beliefs

You may have heard the expression that says that your beliefs determine your results. And I believe there's a lot of truth in that. In other words, if you think that you don't know how to manage money, or even worse, that you don't deserve money, that's what you will get in life. You are not alone. A lot of people struggle with limiting beliefs about money. Most of us didn't get a good education about money. In schools, they don't teach financial intelligence, although they should. The chances are that you've also picked up some negative financial beliefs from your parents. But the good news is that raising your financial IQ can help you get rid of those limiting beliefs. That's the first step to achieving financial abundance.

Smarter, Not Harder

Have you noticed that wealthy people seem to get wealthier every year even if they don't work harder than others? Have you ever wondered what their trick is? Well, there's no trick. It all comes down to high financial IQ and knowing how to manage your money. Raising your financial IQ can help you in multiple ways. First, you must work to realize where your money is going. Next, you can identify unnecessary costs or areas where you can save money. After that, it is time to start making wise choices with the excess. Investing wisely and making good choices is the best way to increase your wealth. The best thing is that you don't have to work harder, you just have to make smarter moves.

Setting Financial Goals

It is nice to have a vision of how you'd like your business or personal wealth to grow, but without clear financial goals, it is hard to make it work. It is essential to learn how to set realistic short- and long-term financial goals and work towards achieving them. Financial goals are not just about the number you want to see on your bank account. Especially if you are a business owner – the situation is far more complex. You are responsible for a larger budget, but also for all people that work for you. You have to look at the bigger picture, and goal setting is essential.

Hiring the Right People

As I already mentioned, you don't have to do everything alone. You don't need to be your own accountant and bookkeeper. I highly recommend delegating these tasks to professionals. However, you need to have basic financial knowledge if you want to hire the right people. Even if you plan to outsource your finances, you still need to raise your financial IQ. This will ensure a great partnership, and you will naturally get more value from your professionals.

Investing Wisely

Some women believe that you need to have a large amount of money before considering investing. I don't agree. That's just one of your limiting beliefs about money. Investing is one of the best ways to multiply your assets. You can invest in different things: real estate, stocks, etc. But the first thing you should invest in is your education and personal growth. Even if your formal education is over, remember that investing in yourself is the best move you can make. Never stop learning. And then, with financial knowledge, you can determine what areas are worth investing in. You should never rely solely on the opinions of others because the right solution for their business might not be right for yours as well.

Becoming Accountable

When you lack financial knowledge, it is easy to blame others: your family, the market, or the government. That happens because you don't understand the power you have when you learn to control your finances. The most successful people are fully accountable for everything they do. Because only when you take full responsibility will you be able to change something in your life. This is true for your finances as well. Raising your financial IQ will allow you to see all the mistakes you've made in the past and avoid repeating them in the future. You will stop blaming others, and you will be ready to make smarter decisions and grow your business.

Learn How to Read Financial Statements

If you've never worked with financial statements, they may seem complicated to you. But they are actually not, and I believe everyone should learn how to read their own financial statements. Even if you have an excellent accountant, you still need this. I think it is an essential part of financial literacy. Let's talk about the basics:

First, every financial statement should have four parts. They include the balance sheet, the income statement, the cash flow statement, and the explanatory notes. The balance sheet shows the assets owned by the entity and the liabilities owed, resulting in the equity that has accumulated. The income statement shows the earnings of the business.

Many people overlook the cash flow statement, but it is essential to know where your money goes. There are a variety of reasons to learn how to read financial statements and understand the terminology. Whether you own your company or choose to invest in a business, financial statements tell you an extraordinary amount of information. Financial statements also include information from the firm that prepared them and just what level of assurance they are providing.

Accounting is a unique combination of art and science. It is not a dull set of rules, as some people believe.

Explaining Generational Wealth

I am sure you've heard of the term generational wealth or family wealth and thought: "Wow. If only I were lucky to have generational wealth!" But why not be the one to start generational wealth in your family? I believe you should make generational wealth one of your long-term goals.

Basically, generational wealth consists of assets that you pass on to the next generations. If you had to struggle starting from scratch, you know how hard it can be. Family wealth has many benefits. For example, it can allow your children to choose the university they want or to start their own business. Some of the most common forms of generational wealth are real estate and stock market investments. Of course, your legacy should also include financial education you can pass to your children.

Once your personal financial plan is set and you are ready for the next step, it will really start to unfold. At that point, you can start working on building your legacy for future generations. Here are some examples:

- **Invest in real estate** – Buying real estate can be one of the best decisions in your life. As soon as you buy your first house, you can start planning your next property. It is essential to choose a location whose value tends to increase over time. Cities are expanding rapidly, and what seems like a suburb today can become an exclusive location tomorrow. It is always a good idea to consult experts who can explain trends in the real estate market.

- **Invest in securities** – The financial market is one of the most rewarding means of growing wealth over the long term. While the stock and bond markets include an element of risk, so do all investments. The financial market is a great way to create wealth that will grow over time.

- **Invest in your kids' education** – One of the best gifts you can give to your kids is quality education. There's a big difference between young adults who start their careers with huge college debts and those whose parents paid for it. If you are able to pay for your kids' college fees, they will be able to start saving as soon as they get their first job instead of working to pay off debts.

- **Invest in a family business** – Instead of passing cash and real estate to your kids, you can give them a profitable business. The family-owned business is a very successful model. If your kids like what you do, you should include them and teach them everything you can. Practical experience is priceless, and you can shape their business minds. But if it turns out your kids don't see themselves in the same business as you, don't despair. It is not the end of the world. When you retire, you can sell your company and leave them funds to create their own business.

Planning Essentials That Can't Wait

Until now, I was talking about some basic aspects of financial intelligence that I believe everyone needs to know. But, as I said, I want this book to be more practical. I've envisioned it as a business book full of helpful tips you can apply as soon as you finish reading. That's why I want to explain three things you can do right now. I like to refer to them as setting the foundation for your financial success. I really encourage you to act now because, as you will see, these actions can bring so much clarity into your life and your business. That said, let's get practical now.

Create Your Financial Plan

Many people go through life without having a precise financial plan, or worse, no plan at all, and I believe that's one of the biggest mistakes you can make. I know that it is impossible to plan your life for the next 10 years in detail, but there is great importance in starting somewhere with a strategy. Even if you decide to change something along the way, you will always have a bigger picture that you can stick to. There are various ways to create a financial plan. The best thing you can do is engage a professional to help you and hold you accountable. Here are a few essential components every financial plan should have:

- **Your goals.** How can you measure your progress if you don't know what your goals are? Try to be as specific as you can. I also suggest using the SMART formula. It means that your goals should be specific, measurable, achievable, realistic, and time-bound.

- **Statement of financial position**. This fancy name simply means listing your assets and liabilities and being aware of your net worth. Clarity is the first step to success. If you want to track your progress, you first need to know where you are starting from. Don't forget to update this document each time when there's a significant change in your net worth.

- **Household Spending**. This statement includes listing income from all sources you have. It should also include the expenses you have on a regular basis. Identify those expenditures that are necessary vs. discretionary.

- **Tax Planning.** You should plan your income tax returns in advance, don't let them take you by surprise. It may be a good idea to consult an accountant who can help you plan so that you not only anticipate your liability but minimize it.

- **Potential problems.** Always be honest with yourself. List your strengths and weaknesses and try to predict any problems or issues that may arise.

- **Risk management.** I am not a pessimist, but I want to prepare myself and my company for difficult times should they arise. Risk management and insurance are the best ways to protect yourself in case of unexpected threats to your financial future.

- **Retirement Plan.** Your retirement plan is something sacred. You need to know how much money you will need for your retirement and how much you need to save every month in order to achieve that goal. This is a cornerstone to your future.

- **Investment Plan.** Based on your situation and your tolerance for risk, an investment advisor can maximize your nest egg.

Understand Life Insurance

There are various kinds of life insurance, but the two largest groups are temporary and permanent. Temporary life insurance, also known as term insurance, lasts only for a specific number of years. Most people purchase temporary insurance for periods from 5 years to 30 years.

On the other hand, permanent insurance covers you till the rest of your life. However, some of them have an age limit, which is usually 100 years. The most common types of permanent insurance are whole life and universal life. Other options include variable life and variable-universal life.

The best thing about permanent insurance is that it works both as a death benefit and savings feature. Not only does the family receive funds if the insurance holder dies, but you could also use it for other purposes. It means you can borrow funds from your own policy, or invest them.

Not everyone needs life insurance. There are many situations, however, that life insurance is meant for. It is not really a tool to create wealth, rather, it is made to provide liquidity in certain circumstances. Examples include paying for funeral expenses, funding a mortgage or other debt at death, buying a deceased business owner's interest in their company, caring for minors after the loss of a guardian, and paying estate taxes.

A great insurance advisor gets to know their customer and just what their actual needs are.

Don’t Ignore Your Estate

Most people don't take care of their estate until they are aging or retiring. That’s wrong in so many ways. You never know what can happen. An estate plan should start early and be revised every couple of years as your life and your family changes. Another common misconception is that estate planning is just for rich people, for millionaires. No. Everyone should address this important topic, and it can also help avoid potential disputes in the future.

So, what is estate planning all about?

The most important decision you have to make is determining who is going to inherit your estate when you are no longer here. It doesn't have to be one person, obviously. But if you want to include more people, that's an additional reason to create your estate plan. Your estate doesn't only include your real estate, although that's the first thing people think about. It also includes funds from your accounts, your car, and furniture. It includes the disposition of every asset and every liability.

When you are a business owner, it gets even more complicated. It is imperative that you decide who you will pass your business on to when you retire or if you become seriously ill. People tend to put off business succession planning because the subject matter is unpleasant. The thought process is difficult, and it may need to change over time. But it is essential to start from somewhere. A well-laid plan can help avoid business interruptions and misunderstandings, and it could also save a lot of time and money.

Those who don't plan ahead could waste a lot of money on court costs and legal fees, as well as additional taxes. In many situations, individuals who do not plan properly set their heirs up for a lot of unintended consequences.

The two most common ways to design your estate are by establishing your will or a living trust. Both have some advantages and disadvantages. An attorney that practices family law and understands estate planning is a great asset to your professional team. Every situation is unique. It is up to you to choose what works for you and your family.

Take Care of Your Wealth

Whether you realize it or not, you are wealthy. You are the woman who recognizes all the things she has and all the amazing potential possibilities. If you are reading this book, you are either wealthy, or you will become wealthy in the future. How do I know? Because I see that you are ready to do whatever it takes. You are on your way to creating your dream business or climbing up the corporate ladder. And sooner or later, the results will come. It is hard to establish the point in which one person becomes financially wealthy. You must start identifying as such. Take care of your assets, starting now. It is never too early to create healthy financial habits. They can only help you grow and succeed. You should begin taking your net worth seriously. The first step is to understand where you are now and what your goals are. The second step is to create a clear financial path to achieve those goals!

CHAPTER 9

Surrounding Yourself with a Dream Team

"Surround yourself with only people who are going to lift you higher." – Oprah Winfrey

I've been in this business for more than three decades. If there's anything I've learned, it is that successful people surround themselves with professionals who can help them succeed. I know that when an entrepreneur starts out, they often need to do many things by themselves. Cost is an important factor, and I understand that. But, over the years, as your business grows, you should hire professionals. Understanding this concept differentiates great leaders from other people. Even if you think you can do it alone, there's a big difference between you and someone who performs a specific role every day. A person who does so can do it on a more professional level, and they know what to look for. They notice details that you may not be able to notice. And I've seen this on a small scale with quarterly strategy sessions. And I've seen it on a really big scale when there's some national level buyout of a company. There has never been a case where the use of the team didn't bring value.

I want to share one of my favorite stories as an example. One contractor that was a great client for many years decided it was time to retire. He had to execute a succession plan. These things never come easy. They'd been negotiating for a couple of years, as is often the case. Then, it became serious, and they established a letter of intent. Quickly, we wanted to make sure that we developed a team to support the seller. And that was one of the best decisions ever.

With the support of our team, the seller was able to manage everything faster, smoother, and with a greater net profit.

We assembled a team of advisors: his CPA, attorney, investment advisor, insurance specialist, and bonding agent and banker all rallied to work as a cohesive group.

Selecting Your Business Advisors – Five Must-Have Professionals

For your financial success, it is always essential to have the right team of advisors. Developing a dream team of advisors is one of the wisest things you can do. Before we start talking about all the cool things advisors can do for you, I'd like to talk about how to choose your advisor. There are many ways to find one. They can come from referrals from other like-minded people. Your mentor or colleague could recommend someone, or you could simply find them on the internet. Naturally, the first thing you will check is their knowledge and references. I suggest selecting someone who has experience in your industry. But I believe that the most important thing about choosing your advisor is chemistry.

You have to ask yourself many questions. Are they going to work well with your other advisors as a team? Are they appropriate for you at this stage of your journey? And will they be appropriate in the next two or three years? Instead of focusing only on your current situation, think about your goals and plans for the future. Just like when you are young and getting your first car and starting a relationship with an insurance company. You want to choose a good company that can help you one day when you have a house and family and more responsibilities. This applies to all advisors along the way. Choose someone sophisticated enough to challenge you to get to the next level. They should be able to take care not only of your current situation but also of your goals in the next couple of years. They should be able to help you get to the next level. You should also be aware that it is possible to outgrow your advisor. Someone who was the right choice a couple of years ago, maybe, doesn't fit your needs anymore. And there's nothing wrong with that.

Accountant

I have a lot to say about the accountant's role as your business advisor. This is something I am certainly passionate about. Unfortunately, most people erroneously see the accountant's role as a glorified historian. The retail CPA goes into a prior period and produces something, or corrects something, or compares some piece of compliance. Those things are necessary for banks and the government as you want to make sure you are doing everything right. It is really critical that you have solid financial statements and income tax returns. But when choosing an accountant for your business, the value comes from actually working in the now. They should be giving you real-time information to run your business, providing insight into what you want to do in the future. Never underestimate the accountant's role in creating a future of success.

Insurance Agent

I suggest looking for an insurance agent with a specialization in your field. You should try to find someone with a demonstrated history, who's already worked for a similar company. Insurance agents can provide specific insights on bonding and working capital, which can be very helpful in the long run. A great insurance agent educates to minimize risk and truly has your interest at heart with a long-term plan for helping you choose the coverages you actually need.

Banker

Your banker is another integral part of your team of professionals. Banking is far more complicated than it seems, and it is always better to have professional help. You will need a banker from the beginning, especially if you want to establish credit or borrow money. There are many ways to structure agreements, and if you don't have a banking background, you won't be able to do it yourself. An experienced banker will be able to give you valuable advice in terms of the life cycle of cash flows in your industry and when and how to use debt.

Lawyer

Some people believe you need a lawyer only when you've done something wrong! What a misconception. A good legal advisor can help you make sure you are doing everything according to the law. Most law-related mistakes in business happen unintentionally. Even if you don't want to break a regulation, you may not even be aware of all rules. Moreover, some of them change often, and you need someone who keeps track of everything. There are so many laws and regulations, so make sure you find a lawyer who already has relevant experience in your industry.

Financial Advisor

A financial advisor, also known as a financial planner, helps you develop goals for your future and a plan on how to reach them. They help create the strategy to get you where you want to be financially. Investing, retirement planning, and estate planning are all things they can quarterback.

It can be very challenging to build your team from scratch. Therefore, if you find a great lawyer or a great accountant, ask them who they know. Maybe they've previously worked with someone who's the right fit for your business. Also, this can be an excellent way to build relationships with people from your industry.

Creating Your In-House Accounting Team

In addition to a great outside accountant, understanding the accounting needs inside of the company is also important. I'd suggest your CPA help determine when each level is necessary based on the size of your business and circumstances. The outline I want to share with you has five levels. These are standards for closely held businesses. Of course, everything depends on the size of your business and the stage you are at. Maybe you don't need them all now, but I suggest you have a look because you will need to grow your accounting team as your business grows.

- Chief Financial Officer – At the top of the hierarchy, there should always be a CFO. A CFO is the senior executive responsible for managing the financial actions of the company. They analyze the company's financial strengths and weaknesses and develop ways to strengthen it. The Chief Financial Officer is responsible for communicating with senior management. Moreover, they are responsible for sharing financial information with important shareholders and investors.

- Controller – Controller is one of the most important financial roles in a company. In theory, they don't have the same level of authority as a CFO, but they are responsible for daily operations. They often have more insights than a CFO, however, and that should not surprise you. They are creating the most important financial reports and helping with annual reports. When there's an external audit, your controller is in charge of gathering all the necessary documents.

- Mid-level Accounting Manager – This role depends on the size of your business. In the beginning, most small businesses don't have middle management yet. When you create middle management, it is time to promote someone as a mid-level accounting manager. This can be one of the biggest turning points in your business. They are responsible for supervising accountants and checking their reports.

- Accountant – Accountant may be low on this hierarchy list, but you should never underestimate their role. They are the ones with direct responsibility for daily tasks such as invoices, payrolls, or reports. As your business grows, you should have one accountant who specializes only in payrolls, the other who works only with invoices, and so on. Some companies also have financial analysts who work closely with an accountant. But in small companies, one person often covers both roles.

- Accounting Clerks – Some people like to call them accounting clerks, while others call them accounting assistants. The idea is the same. They are usually young people, beginners who do entry-level tasks. Some of their tasks can include data entering, processing payroll, as well as the initial number-crunching. However, more experienced staff should always supervise them.

You could establish your in-house accounting hierarchy in a way that everyone has their mentor. This is a good way to train people you trust, so they can move to higher positions as your business grows.

The Power of a Good Team

If you only remember one thing from this chapter, I'd like it to be that having an awesome team is essential for success. We've talked a lot about delegating tasks and focusing only on the areas you are great at. An efficient team can achieve much more than a single professional, no matter how hard they may work. This is even more important when it comes to specific areas like accounting or law. It is always better to leave that part of the work to those who can fully focus on it. But the team is much more than sharing work tasks. If you surround yourself with exceptional people they will help you grow. Every day you can learn something new from each other. They can teach you a lot about having the right attitude, mindset, discipline, or getting your habits right. You are there to inspire and motivate each other. It is a known fact that you can achieve much more when you surround yourself with successful people. They push you and challenge you to grow in ways that you didn't even know possible. Be very careful when choosing your team and then make sure to let them know you appreciate them.

CHAPTER 10

It is Time to Play to Your Strengths

If you've carefully read each chapter of this book, I know you are hungry to achieve extraordinary success. Women often believe they need more knowledge or more skills. This book can open your mind to many strategies and solutions you need, but it is up to you to apply them. I really hope that you are now aware of how powerful women are in business. Our role is very important, and I think it will become even more important. Remember how amazing your potential is, and don't compare yourself to others. Focus on what you do best and do more of it.

The world needs you to do things you are great at. To express your talents and your strengths. For everything else, surround yourself with a great team to help you. No matter how small your team may be initially, your job is to organize and motivate them. You should work on becoming a great leader. And I know you are capable of that. We, women, have many traits that make us excellent leaders. We just need to recognize our strengths and then get the most out of them. Think about all social skills and life skills that you could apply in the business world as well. Maybe you are an excellent communicator? Perhaps you have a high level of emotional intelligence? Maybe you are great at time management and budget planning?

Daily life and business life don't have to be two separate things. Women should strive to create a work/life balance that allows them to be great at both. And believe me, that's possible. I live there, and I know how hard it can be. But when you manage to achieve that balance, you will become unstoppable. And when the unexpected derails your plans, you will be able to get back on track. Because, remember, what is failure? Failure is just a lesson that teaches you something. It is an occasion to learn something so you can be better next time. I don't believe in failures. I think that one can't fail in life or business. You can only give up, and that's not the same thing.

Hopefully, you picked up a few things that will inspire you. The reason I love books so much is that you can always return and maybe read something that you haven't noticed before. If you need help with some particular areas of your business, I'd be glad to help. You can contact my office and explain your situation so I can find the best way to be of service. I believe that women should support each other in all areas, especially in business. And I will be more than happy to use all my knowledge and experience to help you overcome the challenges you are currently facing. There's nothing that we can't solve together.

www.ingramcontent.com/pod-product-compliance
Lightning Source LLC
LaVergne TN
LVHW010623100826
845148LV00014B/3088

* 9 7 8 0 5 7 8 8 4 4 2 7 5 *